D1443837

Exploration
and Settlement

THE MAKING OF AMERICA ★ ★ ★

Exploration *and* Settlement

Richard Steins

RAINTREE
STECK-VAUGHN
RSVP® PUBLISHERS

A Harcourt Company

Austin · New York
www.steck-vaughn.com

Published by Raintree Steck-Vaughn Publishers, an imprint of Steck-Vaughn Company

Developed by Discovery Books
Editor: Sabrina Crewe
Designer: Sabine Beaupré
Maps: Stefan Chabluk

Raintree Steck-Vaughn Publishers Staff
Publishing Director: Walter Kossmann
Project Manager: Joyce Spicer
Editor: Shirley Shalit
Electronic Production: Scott Melcer

Consultant Andrew Frank, California State University, Los Angeles

Library of Congress Cataloging-in-Publication Data
Steins, Richard.
    Exploration and settlement/Richard Steins.
        p. cm. -- (The making of America)
    Includes bibliographical references (p.) and index.
    Summary: Recounts the stories of the French, English, and Dutch in the New World,
    their reasons for settlement, and their relations with the Native Americans.
        ISBN: 0–8172–5700–4
        1. America—Discovery and exploration—European—Juvenile literature. [1.
    America—Discovery and exploration. 2. Indians of North America—History.] I Title. II.
    Making of America (Austin, Tex.)

        E121 S.76   2000
        970.01—dc 21
                                                    99–046961
Printed and bound in the United States of America
1 2 3 4 5 6 7 8 9 0 IP 04 03 02 01 00 99

Acknowledgments
Cover The Granger Collection; p. 6 Corbis; p. 9 Denver Museum of Natural History' pp. 10, 12, 13, 15 Corbis; p 16 Ohio Historical Society; pp. 18, 20, 21, 22, 24, 26, 28 Corbis; p. 30 North Wind Picture Archives; pp. 33, 34 Corbis; p. 35 The New York Public Library; pp. 38, 39 Corbis; p. 40 Library of Congress; pp. 42, 44, 46, 48, 51 Corbis; p. 54 The Granger Collection; pp. 56, 57 Corbis; p. 58 North Wind Picture Archives; p. 61 The Association for the Preservation of Virginia Antiquities; pp. 64, 65 Corbis; p. 66 The Granger Collection; pp. 68, 69 Corbis; p. 70 North Wind Picture Archives; pp. 72, 73, 74, 76, 80, 81, 83 Corbis; p. 84 North Wind Picture Archives; p. 85 University of Delaware; p. 87 Corbis.

Cover illustration: This 1634 colored engraving shows the English navigator Captain Bartholomew Gosnold arriving on the North America shore, at what is now New Bedford, Massachusetts, in May 1602.

Contents

1

Early American Peoples

The story of America's first people is a fascinating mystery. Historians and scientists are still searching for pieces of the ancient puzzle.

Archaeologists learn about the lives of ancient people from the things they leave behind. These pictures were found on the walls of a cave in Mexico. They were painted by early inhabitants of North America.

We do know that human beings existed elsewhere in the world long before they reached North America. Archaeologists, who study life in the distant past, have found the remains of ancient people in Africa, Europe, and Asia. Humans lived in those places for hundreds of thousands of years before any people arrived in the Western Hemisphere.

Why were early humans not found in America? The reason was that the great land mass that makes up North and South America was separated from Europe, Asia, and Africa by large oceans. The first humans appeared in Africa about four to five million years ago. They slowly began migrating throughout Europe and Asia, but could not reach the continents of North and South America.

About 25,000 years ago, humans learned to use needles made of animal

bones to sew animal skins and make warm clothing. This meant that humans could then live in the cold climates of northern Europe and Asia. There they used spears to hunt large animals for food, clothing, and shelter.

Migration to North America

Archaeologists have developed different ideas about when and how the first people came to North America. It is very probable that they came from Asia. We now live in a period when the Earth's climate is fairly warm. But from 80,000 to about 12,000 years ago, much of the northern part of the Earth was covered with ice. During this Ice Age, the sea level dropped in the Bering Sea, which separates the Siberian region of Russia from Alaska. This narrow body of water may have become a large area of land. Over this "land bridge," people from Siberia could have traveled to Alaska.

Creation Myths

Like other ancient societies, Native Americans had myths, or sacred stories, to explain where they came from. There were as many different creation stories as there were different peoples. The stories often told of a great spirit who breathed life into the world. Stories in some tribes, handed down over thousands of years, tell of long journeys made by ancestors to reach their homelands.

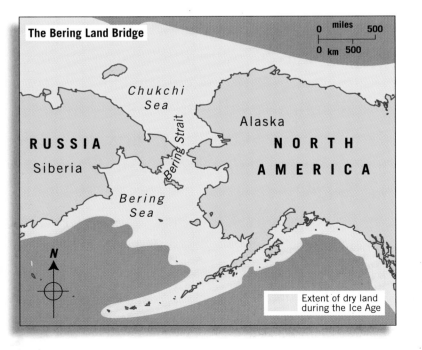

When the water level dropped in the Bering and Chukchi Seas during the Ice Age, a great landmass probably appeared between northeast Asia and the northwest of North America. People and animals could have crossed from one continent to another.

This migration probably occurred several times over a period of many thousands of years. Groups of people gradually traveled from Alaska into Canada, then farther south into what is now the United States. Within a thousand years of the first arrivals from Siberia, their descendants had reached the tip of South America.

The Paleo-Indians

What accounted for this migration? Many scientists believe that these first Americans, later named Paleo-Indians, were hunters in search of the mammoth. Mammoths were large, hairy elephants that are now extinct. These huge animals were a main source of food and skins for clothing and shelter.

Most Paleo-Indians lived in groups of about 15 to 20 people. The men hunted while the women prepared food and cared for the children. Paleo-Indians were usually on the move, looking for mammoths and other large mammals, such as giant bison. They hunted with spearheads that they carved from stone.

The warming of the Earth, however, created a problem for the Paleo-Indian peoples. Large animals became extinct, probably for two reasons. They were not suited to the warmer climate, and they had been hunted faster than they could reproduce. The disappearance of the large mammals forced the early Americans to change their ways of life over time in order to survive.

Archaic Societies

As the Earth warmed, ice melted away and left new environments. Huge forests grew in what is now the eastern United States. In the central part of the country, grassland prairies developed. Deserts formed in the west. In these different landscapes, a rich variety of trees, plants, grasses, animals, and fish slowly appeared.

The early Native Americans changed their ways to suit the new climates, from cold in the north to warmth closer to the equator. People no longer migrated long distances to

"Lo! Even the trees on high mountains near the clouds and Sky-father crouch low towards the Earth-mother for warmth and protection! Warm is the Earth-mother, cold the Sky-father, even as woman is warm, man the cold being!"

From a Zuñi creation legend

follow huge animals. They began to live off smaller animals and fish, and also to collect wild plants for food.

Paleo-Indians were developing into what archaeologists call the Archaic hunter-gatherers. The Archaic period lasted from about 10,000 to 2,000 years ago.

Like their Paleo-Indian ancestors, the Archaic people hunted with spears. They also developed nets, hooks, and traps to collect their prey. To prepare plants and seeds for food, they developed new tools, such as the grinding stone. They made utensils and ornaments from a wide variety of bones, shells, ivory, clay, and leather.

As the climate gradually got warmer, giant ice caps melted, and a body of water rose once again to cover the "land bridge" between Alaska and Asia. The descendants of the early migrants were now permanently in the Americas. The warmer climate meant improved living conditions and greater ease of travel. Gradually, people moved to all parts of North and South America.

George McJunkin's Discovery

George McJunkin was born an African-American slave in Texas in 1851. He was freed in 1865, and became the manager of a ranch near the town of Folsom. In 1908, after a flood on his ranch, McJunkin noticed something unusual in a hole in the ground. A large white bone had been exposed by the flooding. The bone was much bigger than any of the cattle and horse bones McJunkin was used to seeing. He kept the bone, and over the years showed it to anyone who was interested.

After McJunkin's death in 1922, the importance of his discovery became obvious. McJunkin had stumbled on the bones of a giant bison that was more than 10,000 years old.

Scientists found the bones of 23 giant bison near the one McJunkin had discovered. Mixed in with the bones were spear points used by humans to hunt the giant bison. One of the points was stuck in between two bison ribs, where it had been plunged by an ancient hunter thousands of years ago. The spear points were named "Folsom points," and they proved that humans had lived in North America for at least 10,000 years.

As groups settled into particular regions, they had less contact with people in other areas. Over thousands of years, separate languages and traditions took root in different parts of the continents. As people became more settled, regional cultures, or ways of life, developed. This meant that different social groups, or "tribes," began to share languages and ways of life because of where they lived.

Great Plains Bison Hunters

Native American groups in the Great Plains region still tended to move around with the seasons, but now they were in search of plants as much as animals. Plains people did not have permanent villages, but they returned to areas with good sources of food.

Great herds of bison still roamed the grassy Great Plains area east of the Rocky Mountains.

Plains Indians continued to hunt bison for hundreds of years as their ancestors had done. But they began to use bows and arrows instead of spears.

The people in this region hunted on foot, usually in groups, and developed ways of trapping and killing groups of bison. Hunters might stampede several bison into a ravine, where they were trapped and could be speared. Or they would force animals to run in a group over a cliff, where they would be killed or injured in the fall.

Great Plains hunters kept many traditions and rituals that went as far back as the Paleo-Indians. But after about A.D. 550, the Plains hunters developed the bow and arrow. This allowed them to kill bison from a much greater distance than did a spear, which had to be thrown from up close.

Great Basin Peoples

The region between California and the Rocky Mountains is called the Great Basin. Many Archaic hunter-gatherer cultures developed in the different environments there. In areas where rainfall was heavy, marshes and lakes became sources of fish and birds. Archaic people in these areas often made model ducks out of reeds. The models, known as decoys, attracted real ducks and other birds. The birds were then captured by being grabbed or trapped in a net. Archaeologists have found examples of these decoys, some of which are almost 3,000 years old.

Hunters in the Great Basin went after deer and antelope, and also caught snakes, rabbits, and rodents for food. They used nets to trap animals, and sometimes started fires to drive the animals into nets.

The Great Basin peoples also used plants for food. They collected plants and stored them in baskets for long periods to guard against food shortages caused by bad weather. This mixed diet helped people in the region to survive through difficult times.

Pacific Coast Cultures

Archaic Indians in what are now California, British Columbia, and the Pacific Northwest tended to live in permanent settlements. This was because the environment

was rich enough to provide all they needed. People along the Pacific coast were greatly helped by their closeness to the sea. There were many kinds of fish and other sea animals, such as whales and seals. In addition, the fertile land along the coast was a good source of plants, fruit, and nuts. Acorns were an important food to the many hunter-gatherer peoples in the coastal area.

Immediately inland from the Pacific coast, other groups lived in the great canyons and river valleys. The whole region supported many different tribes. By 1500, there were some 90 different languages spoken in the Pacific coast area. The Chumash people of Southern California lived in large settlements of more than a thousand people. They had a system of money based on beads and shells.

Pacific coast peoples north of California lived in fairly large villages, and built houses made of cedarwood. They were expert woodcarvers and made large wooden canoes for fishing. Their large carvings of animals and the spirits of their ancestors came to be known later as totem poles.

Archaic Peoples of the Southwest

Archaic peoples in the Southwest—now Arizona, New Mexico, and parts of Colorado and Utah—developed farming societies. Many lived in pueblos, which were villages of clay dwellings built close together in terraces or into the sides of cliffs.

The Southwest is extremely dry for most of the year. The Archaic Indians who lived here probably started cultivating their own crops because wild plants were not a dependable source of food when there was no rain.

Farming, or agriculture, came relatively late to the Southwest, but its development was very important for all Native Americans. Around 1500 B.C., Southwestern peoples

Totem poles were carved by peoples of the Northwest, such as the Haida and the Tlingit. They were used to mark territory, and as memorials for ancestors and important events.

began to grow a type of corn, which had been brought north from Central and South America. They probably grew corn because it was a sturdy plant that could live in a difficult environment. They also grew squash and beans that had come from Central America. With these three crops, Southwestern peoples no longer had to roam for food, and they gradually settled into villages. All of this did not happen overnight. Small settlements began to emerge between A.D. 200 and 900.

One of the cultures of this early period was that of the Anasazi, who built reservoirs to capture rainwater for irrigation. Later Anasazi peoples built large cliff dwellings with many rooms. Pueblo Bonito, an elaborate structure with more than 800 rooms, can still be seen at Chaco Canyon, New Mexico. The Anasazi left their cliff dwellings around 1200, maybe because a long period without rain destroyed their agriculture. Some Anasazi moved to areas of greater rainfall, where their descendants still live as Zuñi and Hopi peoples.

These ruins of a cliff dwelling are in Mesa Verde National Park, Colorado. Hundreds of Anasazi people lived in the Cliff Palace, as it is now called.

The Gift of Corn

Corn was so important in the diet of most Native American peoples that it held a sacred place in their societies. Seneca people, in what is now New York State, held a yearly corn-planting ceremony to ask the gods for good weather and a successful crop. Others named periods of the year according to parts of the corn harvest :"planting," "weeding," "ripening," and so on.

Indian people were able to produce large amounts of corn with their farming methods. It was a very healthy food and had many uses. It could be eaten as a vegetable or ground into flour to make breads and hot cereal. By 1500 B.C., corn had become the main food crop of people throughout all of North America.

Corn was to become one of the most valuable gifts from Native Americans to later settlers who came from Europe. They also used it as one of their main foods. Nothing went to waste, as pigs and chickens ate corn kernels, and cows ate the stalks and leaves of the plant. By the 1700s, corn formed a huge part of the exports of North America to the rest of the world.

Another Southwestern group, the Mimbres people, made beautiful pottery that showed human and animal forms. The Hohokam people of Arizona made wide use of irrigation. They built large, rectangular-shaped pit houses, which may have been used both for storing food and for ceremonies.

Eastern Woodlands Peoples

The area east of the Mississippi River was heavily forested in early America. From the vast river valleys of the Mississippi and the Ohio to the Atlantic coast on the east, a wide variety of Archaic cultures developed.

Despite their differences, the peoples of the Eastern Woodlands had certain things in common. They all lived near rivers, lakes, or the ocean. They fished with nets and spears and trapped small animals for food. Eastern Woodlands people were all greatly dependent on deer for meat, hides, and bones that were made into tools. They also ate nuts and plants, as did other Archaic peoples.

Some of the ancient burial sites of the Woodlands peoples still exist today. One site in Kentucky, where more than 1,100 burial sites were discovered, is probably about 4,000 years old. Archaeologists worked out that these Woodlands people lived to be little more than 18 years old. A few of the burial sites contained shells, which were used as a form of money. This shows that they traded with other people. Some sites contained the remains of humans who died from spear wounds. This indicates that Woodlands people must have fought each other at times, perhaps over hunting grounds.

John White, an English artist who came to America in 1585, drew this picture of Native Americans fishing in what is now North Carolina. They fished with traps, spears, and nets as their Eastern Woodlands ancestors had done in Archaic times.

Woodlands peoples began to develop agriculture around 2000 B.C., and started to grow corn around 300 B.C. They also grew tobacco, and some burial sites contained pipes for smoking. They made pottery, a skill they may have learned from people farther south.

Woodlands peoples who lived at Poverty Point, in what is now Louisiana, built huge structures made out of earth sometime between 2,500 and 3,500 years ago. Nobody knows why. Perhaps they were used for looking at the sky and stars, or as meeting places for traders. They were shaped like half-circles and measured more than 2,500 feet (760 meters) wide. Thousands of people lived in smaller dwellings around these massive structures.

"Their bread is Indian corn beaten to pieces between two stones, of which they make a cake, and bake it in the ashes. Their other victuals are venison, turkeys, hares, bears, wildcats . . . . The fish they cook just as they get them out of the water without cleansing."

Letter about Native Americans from a Dutch settler in the 1640s

Burial Mound Cultures

Around 500 B.C., Woodlands peoples began to build burial mounds. Archaeologists believe that a society ruled by chiefs had developed, because these imposing structures must have been intended for very important people.

Hundreds of burial mounds have been found near Chillicothe, Ohio, built between 500 B.C. and 100 B.C. by the Adena peoples. The dead were often buried with a variety of items, including spear points, pipes, ornaments, headdresses, and sometimes even the polished skull of an enemy or ancestor.

In about 100 B.C., the Adena culture changed into the Hopewell culture. The Hopewell built even larger mounds, filling them with more and more items. Some of the Hopewell mounds were shaped like animals. The Serpent Mound in Ohio, for example, is shaped like a snake and is more than 1,200 feet (360 meters) long. The objects found inside the burial mounds, such as jewelry made from bear teeth and pearls, show what fine craftspeople the Hopewell people were.

The Serpent Mound in Ohio was built by the Hopewell people. This aerial photograph clearly shows its snakelike shape.

Despite the different ways of life that developed in the Archaic period, and the huge distances between groups, Native American people kept certain systems of belief and ways of living that were similar in most regions.

Family and Clan Communities

The most important social groups within Native American tribes were the family, the clan, and the village. Although there were exceptions, most people lived in families, and related families formed a larger group called a clan. Depending on the particular culture, clan membership could be passed down from either the father or the mother. Clans served the purpose of linking widely scattered groups within a tribe. Several clans usually lived together in a village. Membership in a clan was sometimes even more important than an immediate family.

Couples usually married when they were in their teens. Except for people in the Southwest, women farmed and took care of children, while men hunted, fished, traded, and defended the tribe. Iroquois women in the New York area owned the fields as a group and made decisions in the tribal councils. In the Southwest, men and women shared agricultural labor. Land was owned by the whole group in pueblo communities, and clan membership passed down through the mother's family.

Beliefs and Values

Almost all Native American groups believed that they were just one part of a balanced, natural world. They believed that nature was alive with spiritual power. This idea was, and still is, at the center of Native American

Cahokia

About A.D. 800, a burial mound culture called the Mississippians arose in the central and southeastern parts of North America. The Mississippians built a huge site at Cahokia, Illinois, where more than 100 mounds can still be seen. The site spread for six square miles (15 sq km), and at its center was an enormous four-terraced structure.

This site may at one time have been a large settlement of over 30,000 people. In the region around Cahokia were numerous cities, towns, and farming villages. Cahokia was the center of a vast trading network. Archaeologists have found evidence in Cahokia of great social differences. There was a worker class that did the backbreaking labor, a class of managers, and religious leaders at the top.

Mississippian culture lasted for about 700 years, and nobody is sure why it ended. Large settlements gave way to small communities, where people hunted and farmed. When the French explorer La Salle passed through the region in 1682, the site of Cahokia was a small village, with no sign of the great settlement that had been in the area centuries before.

The shamans were important people in Native American communities. They were leaders and healers as well as holy men. This shaman is performing a ceremony to conjure up the spirits of ancestors.

religions. Their belief in supernatural powers meant that people saw spiritual forces in nature, in things such as water and rocks, the moon and sun, and in living things. They often prayed to the spirits of the animals they hunted.

Early American religions tried to satisfy evil spirits that could bring illness and death. Some peoples, the pueblo groups for example, also performed frequent rituals of gratitude. They would give thanks for things such as rainfall that was so important for their crops.

In order to communicate with the spirits, Native Americans relied on special holy men, sometimes known as shamans. Many holy men were also healers who used medicinal plants and magic to cure ailments. Shamans took charge of rituals, such as the coming of age celebrations for young men and women, and they played a major role in tribal councils.

Children were raised to respect the community and to cooperate with the wishes of the group. This behavior was essential for everyone's survival. Indian parents rarely spanked their children, but they could threaten them with being "outcasts," which meant being expelled from the tribe and dying alone in the wilderness. In North American societies, the good of the tribe came first. Decisions were made as a group, and the leaders depended on the respect of their people.

Travel and Trade

Native Americans in North America engaged in trade with groups all over the continent. Trade was important not only as a way of getting goods, but as an exchange of ideas and

Native American Culture Areas and Major Tribes

skills. It was also a way of showing and gaining respect in dealings with other peoples.

Many materials for tools, utensils, and ornaments were obtained by Archaic peoples through trading with other tribes, both near and far. Archaeologists have discovered seashells from coastal regions hundreds of miles inland. These shells could well have been used in the exchange of goods, and show that Archaic peoples were able to travel far from their homelands in search of trade.

How did they travel over such distances? There were no horses in North America at the time. Most Archaic people probably traveled by water, along the rivers, lakes, and even the oceans. They made simple, one-person boats from rawhide or bark, and larger boats from hollowed-out cedar logs. The larger boats could travel on the oceans

When Europeans arrived in North America in the late 1400s, a huge number of Native American communities had been long established in their tribal homelands.

along the coast, and were a speedy way of getting from one point to another.

In the Southwest, wide, straight roads extended out of Chaco Canyon in New Mexico. These may have been trading routes for the Anasazi who traveled on foot. They had an extensive trade in pottery, baskets, and shells.

The Adena and Hopewell peoples traded with other peoples at great distances. Hopewell graves contained items from as far away as Canada and Florida. Hopewell goods, from what is now Ohio, have in turn been found in the Southwest.

Native Americans traveled long distances to trade goods and materials with peoples in other areas. Cooking utensils, tools, and baskets were common trade items.

The First Americans

There is no way to know exactly how many people were living in North and South America before Europeans started to arrive. Historians are still debating the figure today. Some believe the number may have been as high as 80 million, and that up to 10 million lived in North America. We do know that people lived in every area of the Americas. Many societies and cultures existed and thrived, from large settlements to small traveling groups. Hundreds of tribes spoke many different languages. In fact more languages were spoken in North America than in Europe at the time.

2

Europe's Age of Exploration

Long before they knew of the Americas, people in Europe were trying to learn more about the world. For centuries, they had explored the East—that is, the Middle East and Asia, including India and China. In the process, they expanded their knowledge and skills. They learned how to make long voyages across vast and dangerous seas.

Christian Europeans came to the Middle East as pilgrims, to worship at holy sites, but also to try and conquer the Muslims.

The Lure of the East

In 1096, Europeans began a centuries-long effort to capture the Middle East. The East was the historic birthplace of Christianity, and the Europeans wanted to take it from the Arabs, who were Muslims. The Crusades, as these efforts were known, all failed in the end to defeat the Muslims.

However, Europeans developed a profitable trade in goods with the East. They sold their cloth in return for Eastern goods such as spices. Spices were important to Europeans, who used them to preserve food, particularly meat, and to make their food taste better. They also traded for silk, ivory, gold, and carpets, all of

21

The Astrolabe

Some form of astrolabe was probably invented by the ancient Greeks, who used it to measure the movements and positions of planets and stars. In the 1400s, the astrolabe was a useful navigation tool on voyages of discovery. Sailors used it to determine latitude, longitude, and time of day.

A simple astrolabe was a disk with its circumference marked off in degrees. At its center was a movable pointer. By sighting the pointer and taking readings of its position on the circle, distances could be worked out. Some astrolabes were quite elaborate, with star maps and signs of the zodiac added as decoration.

which were in great demand by Europeans who could afford them. These goods were carried overland from as far away as India and Persia through the Middle East, on their way to the wealthy households of Europe.

The Renaissance in Europe

As they looked beyond their own countries, Europeans sought new information about the world they lived in. This desire for knowledge was part of a huge cultural change, known as the Renaissance, that took place in Europe from the 14th to 16th centuries. Europeans of the Renaissance were most interested in commerce, art, and science.

Scientists at the time were especially interested in the work of ancient Greek geographers and Arab mathematicians. By the 1400s, many people believed, as had the ancient Greeks, that the Earth was a sphere. The question was, how large was this sphere?

Their interest in this question led Europeans to draw more accurate maps. The art of mapmaking and study of the stars became important tools in their long sea journeys. These skills made it possible for sailors to work out their locations, even when out of sight of land.

As trade with the East developed, the need for transportation led to the building of better ships. Trading was originally controlled by Italian city-states such as Venice and Genoa. Ships from the Middle East would travel west through the Mediterranean Sea and dock in the ports of these cities. Goods would then travel by land to other parts of Europe.

In the 1200s, however, ships from Genoa began traveling through the Strait of Gibraltar into the North Atlantic and sailing directly to ports in northern Europe. This was much less expensive than taking goods overland.

Travel in the North Atlantic, however, required ships that could carry heavy cargoes for long distances in stormy seas. Such ships were as useful for exploration as they were for trade.

> "I was curious about finding out things which were hidden from other men, and secret."
>
> *Henry the Navigator*

The Portuguese Lead the Way

In the early 1400s, Portugal was a relatively small and poor country ruled by a group of noble families. Because it faced the Atlantic Ocean, Portugal did not take part in the profitable Mediterranean trade with the Middle East and Asia. But the Portuguese devoted far more energy and money to exploration during the 1400s than all the other countries of Europe combined. Their government actively supported exploration. Its main champion was Prince Henry the Navigator, the son of King Henry of Portugal. Prince Henry encouraged explorers to take risks and sail farther than they had ever journeyed before. He was also interested in increasing Portugal's wealth through trade. To achieve this he looked south, toward the west coast of Africa.

In the 1400s, Europeans had no idea how big Africa was. What they did know was that it contained the possibility of wealth, especially gold. Gold was the basis of the money used in European trade. As trade increased, more and more gold was needed. Gold mined in West Africa passed through the

Prince Henry (1394–1460) and the Caravels

Prince Henry the Navigator's support for exploration expanded European knowledge of geography, navigation, and the African continent. He founded an observatory where people studied the stars, and a school for the study of geography and navigation. Between 1444 and 1446, more than 40 ships sailed for the coast of western Africa under Henry's orders. His navigators reached the Senegal River, the Madeira Islands, and even as far as Sierra Leone.

The ships used to explore over these vast distances were small by today's standards.

Prince Henry at his observatory in Portugal.

Caravels were first used by Portuguese navigators in the 1400s, and played an important part in the exploration of Africa. The caravels' shallow design meant that they were excellent for exploring close to the shore, and their triangular sails made them easy to steer. But their size limited the amount of food and fresh water that could be carried. As journeys became longer, some sailors preferred larger ships. In the 1500s, the Portuguese and Spanish developed bigger and more advanced ships for crossing oceans.

Sahara Desert to the western Mediterranean. The Portuguese wanted gold and also crops, such as wheat (which was grown in Morocco).

Sailing from Portugal down the west coast of Africa was dangerous, but Portuguese sailors slowly learned how to take advantage of the currents and winds in this region. By 1434, they had reached the northern edge of the Sahara Desert, and in 1444 arrived at Cape Verde. By the late 1400s, the Portuguese were able to navigate as far south as the coast of central Africa.

Wherever they sailed in Africa, the Portuguese built trading outposts along the coast. From these settlements, they traded with the powerful African societies, such as the Wolof and the Obas, that controlled the interior regions. They bartered for slaves, gold, and ivory, and by the 1460s had begun to use African slaves to work sugar plantations in the Cape Verde Islands.

In the late 1400s, the Portuguese began moving farther and farther south along the west coast of Africa. In 1488, the explorer Bartolomeu Días reached the Cape of Good Hope at the extreme southern tip of Africa. The Portuguese now realized that it might be possible to sail around the southern tip of Africa and travel in a northeasterly direction toward Asia.

In 1498, this was achieved by the navigator Vasco da Gama. A new sea route to the East had been opened up, avoiding Mediterranean travel. Portugal gained immediate wealth in the spice trade from Vasco da Gama's first voyage to India, and soon founded trading posts in India, China, and other parts of Asia.

The vast empire built by the Portuguese was based on money. But in the process of building it, they had also made great steps forward in science and technology. Other explorers would soon use this knowledge as they turned their eyes toward the vast Atlantic Ocean and what lay westward beyond the horizon.

Slavery in Africa

Slavery was a fact of life in West Africa long before the arrival of Europeans. Leaders of African empires and individual families relied on slaves. But it was European and Muslim outsiders who made African slavery an international business and tore people from their native societies.

Muslims from North Africa traded horses for slaves. Later, the Portuguese traded for slaves and local products with Africans, often in exchange for gold. The Portuguese slavers changed West Africa, and African kingdoms grew rich providing slaves to the Portuguese. Prince Henry the Navigator banned the kidnapping of African slaves in 1455, but his orders did little to stop the growth of the slave trade.

The use of slave labor on European-owned plantations would later cross to the Americas, creating generations of victims and many more conflicts in years to come.

3

The Arrival of the Europeans

The Vikings, or Norse people, lived in Scandinavia, the part of northern Europe that is now Norway, Denmark, and Sweden. They fished and hunted, and they were warriors. Above all, they were among the best shipbuilders and sailors the world has ever known.

The Norse people left their homelands because of overpopulation, internal quarrels, and a desire for trade and adventure. In the 9th century, Vikings began to raid the coasts of the British Isles and Europe. They were much feared by other Europeans, who dreaded their fierceness and appetite for conquest. The Vikings ventured westward across the Atlantic as far as Iceland in the 870s. From there, in about 980, Vikings under their leader Eric the Red sailed farther west to Greenland, where they built several fishing settlements.

The Vikings Sail to Newfoundland

Around the year 1000, a group of Vikings under Leif Ericsson, the son of Eric the Red, reached the island that is now Newfoundland, in Canada. They were probably the first Europeans to land on the North American continent. They founded a small settlement that they revisited from time to time. Although the Viking ships were sturdy, the journey across the North Atlantic was very dangerous, especially when the seas were churned by howling storms and choked by icebergs.

Historians believe that Leif Ericsson landed on the northernmost tip of Newfoundland. In 1963, the remains of a Viking settlement were unearthed there, at L'Anse aux Meadows (above).

After some ten years, the Vikings stopped visiting Newfoundland. Their expeditions, however, have been kept alive in stories known as the Norse sagas. The sagas are probably mixtures of fact and myth, but they give a picture of the Norse explorations in these early years.

Columbus's Adventures

Christopher Columbus was an Italian explorer who was very interested in the size of the Earth. Many scientists in the late 1400s thought that the Earth was too large for them to sail around in a westward direction and reach the East. Columbus did not believe this. He based his own calculations on a number that had originally been worked out by a medieval Muslim astronomer. Columbus believed, incorrectly, that the circumference of the Earth was only about 16,000 miles (25,600 km). In fact this estimate was about 9,000 miles (14,500 km) short.

Columbus thought that a westbound voyage to Asia, across the Atlantic, would be shorter than traveling east. He tried for several years to persuade King Ferdinand and Queen Isabella of Spain to pay for an expedition to prove this. In 1492, they finally agreed. Columbus sailed with 90 men on three ships from the port of Palos, Spain, August 3, 1492. The ships were the *Niña*, the *Pinta*, and the *Santa Maria*. Columbus himself commanded the *Santa Maria*. On August 12, the fleet reached the Canary Islands.

The ships set sail again on September 6. At first the winds were good, but during the last ten days of the voyage, the ships had periods of no wind at all. Finally, on October 12, the sailors sighted land.

The Arrival of Columbus

Columbus truly believed he had reached Asia. In fact, he had landed in what is now the Bahamas, probably on Watling's Island. Columbus and a group of sailors rowed toward the

Christopher Columbus lands on the island he named San Salvador. At first, he praised the intelligence and customs of the native people. But he soon introduced a forced labor system on the islands he conquered, and shipped thousands of Indians to Europe as slaves.

shore. When they landed, Columbus claimed the land for Ferdinand and Isabella and named it San Salvador (for "the savior," Jesus Christ).

The inhabitants of the island had gathered to look at the three strange ships anchored offshore. Columbus assumed he was somewhere in the East Indies, and that the people who greeted him on the shore were *yndinos*, or "Indians." But they were not what he was expecting. The peoples of the East, he believed, would be wearing fine fabrics such as silk and have on precious jewels. These people wore simple clothing and painted their bodies with different colors. They were friendly to Columbus and his men, and everyone soon exchanged gifts to show their peaceful intentions.

Christopher Columbus (c.1451–1506)

The details of Christopher Columbus's early life are a mystery, but it is generally believed that he was born in Genoa, Italy, in 1451. From the age of 14, Columbus journeyed back and forth across the Mediterranean on trading ships. In 1476, he moved to Lisbon in Portugal, where he married Felipa Moniz, a woman whose father had been a close friend and advisor to Prince Henry the Navigator.

From the Moniz family, Columbus inherited all sorts of maps and charts containing information about currents and winds in the Atlantic. Over the years he studied them, and he learned firsthand about the Atlantic by sailing along the coast of Africa.

After his expedition of 1492, Columbus returned to a hero's welcome in Spain. He later crossed the Atlantic several more times in search of gold and slaves. Between 1493 and 1496, Columbus traveled to Dominica and Hispaniola, where he and his men fought and enslaved many of the native people. Another journey, begun in 1498, took him to the South American mainland. He was accused of cruelty toward natives and Spanish settlers, and returned in disgrace to Spain from Hispaniola in 1500. He was later pardoned and made one last voyage, into the Gulf of Mexico, from 1502 to 1504.

Columbus died in Valladolid, Spain, on May 20, 1506.

The people that Columbus named Indians called themselves Tainos, a word in their language that meant "noble." Tainos were agricultural people who grew corn, potatoes, and tobacco, among other crops. They traveled from island to island in large canoes made from hollowed out logs. Tainos villages had houses that were made of wood with straw roofs.

During their long history in the Caribbean, the Tainos had at times battled with other groups, especially the Caribs, who lived on nearby islands. Their weapons were wooden spears, and the Tainos marveled at Spanish weaponry, which was made of iron.

After a month or so, Columbus grew frustrated with the Tainos people. Communication was extremely difficult. In addition, Columbus soon discovered that they did not possess the riches for which the East was fabled. He was especially interested in finding gold, of which the Tainos had only small quantities.

For several months, Columbus went from island to island, hoping to find an Asian ruler like the emperor of Japan. From October 27 to December 5, 1492, he explored the northeastern coast of Cuba. Columbus's next stop was the island he named Hispaniola, which today is made up of Haiti and the Dominican Republic. There he established an outpost called La Navidad. Columbus began his journey home in January 1493. On board were seven Tainos, proof to his masters that he had indeed found land and people on his westward voyage. He left 39 Spanish men behind on Hispaniola.

After two months, Columbus arrived back in Spain. Ferdinand and Isabella were overjoyed about his discoveries, which they believed would make Spain an even greater power. They made Columbus a nobleman and appointed him governor of the islands he had explored.

Later in 1493, Columbus left on his second trip westward. This time he had 17 ships and more than 1,000 men in his expedition. On his arrival, he discovered that the men he

"They should be good and intelligent servants. . . . and I believe that they would become Christians very easily, for it seemed to me that they had no religion."

Christopher Columbus in his diary, describing his impression of Tainos Indians, 1492

"This island and all others are very fertile to a limitless degree. There are birds of many kinds, and fruits in great diversity. In the interior there are mines and metals, and the population is without number."

Columbus's impressions of Hispaniola, 1493

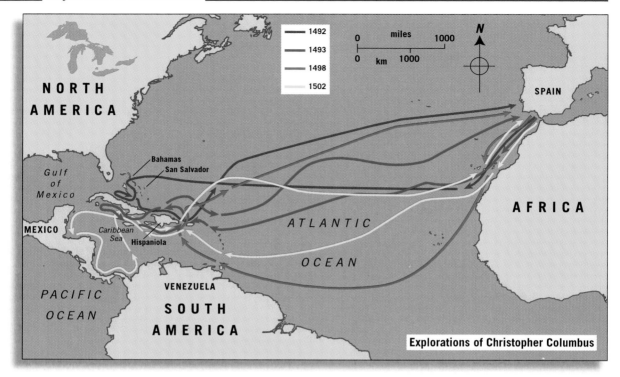

Explorations of Christopher Columbus

Legend:
- 1492
- 1493
- 1498
- 1502

This map shows the routes of Columbus's voyages to the Americas, and where he probably landed on his first journey in 1492.

had left on Hispaniola were all dead. They had treated the Tainos people badly, and the Tainos chiefs had executed them. Columbus left behind more Spaniards to start new settlements and, he hoped, discover great quantities of gold. The settlers, however, quarreled among themselves and were also cruel to the Tainos. These early relations between Europeans and the people already living in the Americas were a bad sign of things to come.

The "New" Continent

It was several years before Europeans understood what Columbus's journeys meant. The knowledge of his adventures spread through the royal courts of Europe, but they were not known to the average person. The people that did know about his journeys generally believed that Columbus had found a shorter route to Asia. Some European rulers were determined not to let Spain seize all the wealth and power that this apparent discovery promised.

Just five years after Columbus's first trip, King Henry VII of England hired an Italian-born trader and sailor named John Cabot to see if he could find a passage to India across the North Atlantic. Cabot set sail in 1497 in a tiny ship, the *Matthew*, from Bristol in England, with a crew of 18. After several weeks, Cabot arrived at Cape Breton Island, now in Canada, and the nearby island of Newfoundland, where the Vikings had been about 500 years before. Like Columbus, Cabot believed he was somewhere in Asia. The next year, 1498, Cabot set out on a second voyage with two ships and 300 men. He intended to sail down the coast he had explored before, hoping to find Japan. Instead, he arrived at a rocky coast which he named Labrador. In later years, England would base its claims to North American territory on Cabot's explorations.

This artist's conception of a forbidding northern landscape shows John Cabot (center, with flag) and his son Sebastian (left) arriving at Newfoundland in June, 1497. Cabot claimed the area for the English king, Henry VII.

In 1498, Columbus landed in what is now the country of Venezuela, in South America. He had no idea that he had landed on a separate continent. That knowledge came from the writings of an Italian navigator named Amerigo Vespucci, who claimed to have explored the South American coast in the late 1400s and early 1500s. Employed first by Spain, and then by Portugal, Vespucci apparently came to the understanding that he had arrived at a "new" continent.

In 1507, Vespucci's claim was put into a new map by a German map-maker named Martin Waldseemüller.

The first name of Amerigo Vespucci (left) was translated into Latin as "Americus." The "Land of Americus" soon became generally known as "America."

Amerigo Vespucci (1454–1512)

Amerigo Vespucci, the Italian navigator in whose honor America is named, was born in Florence, Italy. He started work for the Medici family and in 1492 moved to Seville, Spain. In a letter printed in 1505, he claimed to have made four voyages to the Americas. In the first, which he dated 1497, he said that he explored the South American coast. This would have made him the first European to land on the American mainland.

Most historians think Vespucci's claim is untrue. Perhaps he did go on a Spanish expedition (that of Alonzo de Ojeda) to South America in 1499. In 1501 and 1503, he probably sailed with Portuguese expeditions to the southern coast of South America. But it is unlikely that he ever commanded an expedition himself. Vespucci died of malaria in Spain in 1512.

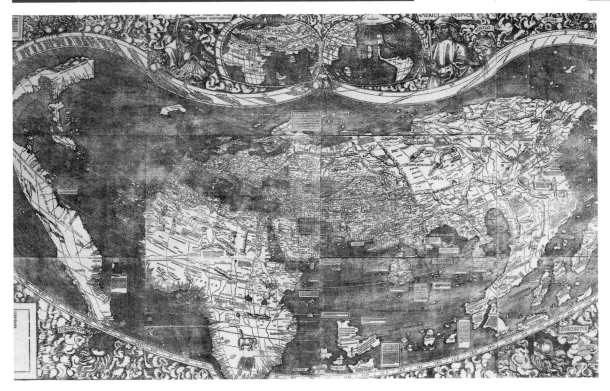

This important map showed for the first time "new lands" that were not connected to Europe, Africa, or Asia. In honor of Vespucci, Waldseemüller named these lands America, for "Amerigo the Discoverer." This resulted in one of those strange events of history: the naming of the Americas after a nearly unknown Italian merchant and seaman.

Two other expeditions proved Vespucci's claims. In 1510, the Spaniard Vasco Núñez de Balboa sailed to Panama, where he took command of the Spanish army based there. Unlike many Spanish explorers, Balboa won the friendship of some Native American people, and enlisted their help when he crossed Panama in 1513. In September of that year, Balboa reached the Pacific Ocean. He realized that this expanse of water must lie between America and Asia.

In 1519, Ferdinand Magellan, a Portuguese navigator working for Spain's King Charles I, attempted to sail completely around the world. In 1520, Magellan sailed

This is a map of the world drawn by Martin Waldseemüller in 1507. It shows (far left) a new continent that was named America after the explorer Amerigo Vespucci.

35

around Cape Horn, at the tip of South America, into the vast ocean that lay to the west. His four-month trip across was so peaceful that he named the ocean "Pacific." Magellan himself never completed his round-the-world expedition. After landing in what are now the Philippines, he was killed in a conflict with natives in 1521. However, a handful of Magellan's original party continued westward through the Indian Ocean and returned to Spain in 1522.

Magellan's expedition was one of the most important in the history of European exploration. He proved that it was possible to sail around the Americas into the Pacific Ocean and to reach Asia. The Strait of Magellan at the southern tip of South America is named for him.

Europeans now knew that there was a separate continent and another ocean to cross before the East could be reached by sailing west from Europe. The old routes from Europe were shorter and faster. So the focus shifted away from finding "routes to the East," and onto America itself.

"Indian Weed"

When Christopher Columbus arrived at San Salvador, one of the gifts he received from the inhabitants was a type of dried leaf. The leaf, which became known as tobacco, was smoked or chewed by the native people, who believed it had health-giving properties.

When Europeans first discovered tobacco, they too believed it was good for them. It certainly failed to bring health, but it became important in the development of European and American civilizations. Smoking and chewing "Indian weed" spread rapidly throughout Europe. Later, tobacco became one of the major cash crops in the English Chesapeake colonies of North America.

Not all Europeans liked the new fad, however. King James I of England called tobacco "hateful to the nose, harmful to the brain, [and] dangerous to the lungs." The king's understanding was far ahead of his time.

4

The Spanish in the Americas

The Spanish had come to the Americas looking for a route to Asia. But they had also come as conquistadors, meaning "conquerors." From their earliest meetings with native American people many Europeans felt they were inferior. They were also seen as a useful workforce, ready to be exploited.

At his settlement on Hispaniola, Columbus began exporting Indian people to Europe to become slaves. He also granted his men the right to demand slave labor from the natives. As the years went by, more Spanish settlers arrived in the Caribbean and on the American mainland. The conquest of native inhabitants became a way of life.

The Spanish Invasion

One of the main goals of the conquistadors was to find gold. And one of the most greedy and ruthless conquistadors was Hernán Cortés. He had come to the Americas in 1504 at the age of 19 in search of adventure and riches. In 1519, the Spanish governor of Cuba sent Cortés on an expedition to the American mainland. He was told to look for an Indian kingdom somewhere in the interior, a fabled place that was supposed to be full of riches.

There was indeed an impressive kingdom in Mexico at the time. The civilization of the Aztecs was ruled from the city of Tenochtitlán by the emperor Montezuma.

When word of Cortés's approach reached the Aztec people, some of them believed that the visitors might be the ancient gods of legend sent from heaven. They offered

"We Spaniards have a disease of the heart which only gold can cure."

Cortés to Montezuma in 1520

The Aztecs under their emperor Montezuma (right) ruled over many Indian tribes. When the Spanish arrived, these tribes rose up against the Aztecs in support of Hernán Cortés (left), who had come looking for gold and glory.

peace and friendship to Cortés and his men. Cortés, however, had not come to make peace with the Aztecs. By 1521, he and his men had overthrown Montezuma's empire. On the ashes of Tenochtitlán, Cortés began to build Mexico City.

Disease and Destruction

How could a few hundred men so quickly overpower such a powerful empire as that of Montezuma and the Aztecs? One reason was that the Spanish were fiercely determined to find gold and had no doubts about the rights and wrongs of what they were doing. Another reason was that they found allies among the peoples who had been conquered by the Aztecs. With their far better weapons, the Spanish were able to overcome large numbers of Aztec people.

But the biggest killers of the native people were diseases brought from Europe. Smallpox and measles made Europeans sick but did not always kill them. However, they were fatal for Indians who had not been exposed to the illnesses before. So quickly did these diseases spread among the Aztecs that their society was completely destroyed. Everyone was affected, even those who didn't get sick. Thousands of people starved to death as trade and food supplies were cut off. In some places, whole villages perished at once.

Montezuma and the Aztecs

When Montezuma came to power in 1502, the Aztec empire was at its biggest and at the height of its power. The Aztec capital was the great city of Tenochtitlán, inhabited by more than 300,000 people. Tenochtitlán was larger than most European cities. It had fresh water, magnificent buildings, and busy craft industries.

The Aztecs' power was based on a system of "tribute." This meant that peoples who were conquered by the Aztecs were required to pay them a tax, or tribute, in return for protection. In this way, the Aztecs governed over millions of people. They were harsh rulers, and this fact helped the Spaniards to overthrow the Aztecs, because they had great support from the empire's Indian victims.

The city of Tenochtitlán.

The first Spaniards to meet the emperor Montezuma were invited to dine with him. One Spaniard described the marvelous feast, in which servants "cooked more than three hundred plates of food." Everything from turkeys, pheasants, partridges, quail, and duck to venison, wild boar, hare, and rabbits was brought to the table. Montezuma was particularly fond of a frothy, chocolate drink served to him in cups made of pure gold.

Montezuma welcomed the Spaniards to the capital city of Tenochtitlán in 1519. He thought Cortés might be a descendant of the god Quetzal. It was a fatal mistake. Cortés took the emperor prisoner and established the city as headquarters for the Spanish conquest of the valuable Aztec land.

In 1520, Cortés left Tenochtitlán for a short time. On his return thousands of Aztecs attacked his army. Cortés brought out Montezuma to quiet the people, but they threw stones at the emperor and seriously wounded him. Montezuma died a few days later, and his successor soon surrendered to the Spaniards. Thus the great Aztec empire ended.

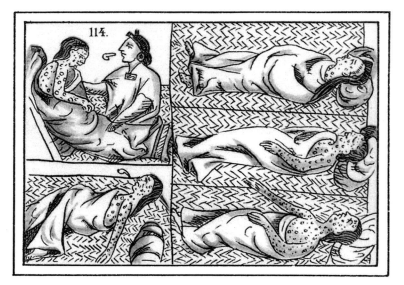

When the Spanish arrived in Mexico and Central America, diseases began to kill the native people. This drawing shows Aztec people suffering from smallpox.

"Broken spears
lie in the roads;
We have torn our
hair in our grief.
The houses are
roofless now . . .
And the walls are
splattered with
gore . . .
We have pounded
our hands in despair
Against the adobe
walls."

Mourning poem of the Aztec

When Cortés landed in 1519, there were probably about 25 million people living in central Mexico. By the early 1600s, that number had been reduced to between 1 and 2 million. This was mostly due to disease, but warfare, starvation, and forced labor also killed many. In the West Indies, entire island populations were wiped out within 50 years. And, in later years, the spread of illness greatly reduced the native population of North America north of Mexico and helped Europeans to settle on Indian land.

The "Columbian exchange" is the name that has been given to the meeting of the two cultures. It refers to whatever went back and forth between the Americas and the rest of the world after the arrival of Columbus. The European diseases that killed millions of Native Americans were part of the Columbian exchange.

The Spanish Empire

Cortés's conquest of the Aztecs was the beginning of the creation of "New Spain." New Spain was the name given to a huge part of the Spanish empire in the Americas, including the areas that are now Florida, the southwestern United States, Mexico, Central America, and the northern part of South America. Cortés himself extended his conquest by sending expeditions over most of Mexico and Central America between 1521 and 1526.

In the 1540s, the Spanish started to mine silver in Mexico and in Peru in South America. Much of this precious metal went to Spain, where the rulers used it to pay their armies. Throughout the 1500s, Spanish conquistadors expanded their

The Columbian Exchange

The term "Columbian exchange" covers many things other than illness. Europeans introduced animals such as horses, cattle, sheep, pigs, and chickens. Crops brought to the Americas included wheat, coffee, and sugarcane. American gifts to Europeans included food crops like corn, potatoes, tomatoes, peanuts, and vanilla. Many plants used as medicines by Native Americans were also taken to Europe.

These exchanges did not occur overnight, however. Europeans, for example, did not eat tomatoes until the 1800s, and Indians at first had to be forced to grow wheat. But over time, the exchange of crops between the two worlds improved the diets and health of people on all continents. Historians believe this is why the world's population doubled over a period of 300 years.

Above all, the Columbian exchange meant a vast, new source of wealth for Europeans. This wealth had an enormous effect on all of Europe, and on the rest of the world through Europe's increasing power.

control into the western part of South America, into what are today Venezuela, Colombia, Peru, Bolivia, Chile, and parts of Argentina. (The northeastern coast of South America, which is now Brazil, was claimed by Portugal.)

The conquistadors were after personal wealth as well as riches for Spain. They were allowed to keep what they conquered, but they had to give one-fifth of their wealth to the rulers. Native peoples now paid tribute to their new masters. They were forced to work for the Spanish. If they refused, they could be punished, enslaved, and even killed.

Throughout the Spanish empire in the Americas, the Roman Catholic Church tried to convert the original inhabitants to Christianity. Franciscan monks arrived in Mexico in 1524, and they were followed by other religious orders during the rest of the century. The monks and priests tended to be less cruel than the conquistadors. Although some of them used whippings to control people, many were also horrified at the treatment of the Indians.

"They picked up the gold and fingered it like monkeys. Their bodies swelled with greed. They hungered like pigs for that gold."

Indian witness describing Spaniards' reaction to gifts of gold from the Aztec, 1519

By the mid-1500s, the Spanish crown had begun taking more and more control of New Spain. The conquistadors had set up estates and silver mines, and had almost complete control of the Indians. Now they began to lose much of that control. The Spanish kings collected tribute that before had gone to local conquerors. Despite this change, life for the native population altered very little.

In the 1500s, Spanish settlers made up about one to two percent of New Spain's population. Most of them were male, and many married Indian women. The children of Spanish men and Indian women were called mestizos, which came from the Spanish word for "mixed."

The Effects of the Spanish Conquest

For the Indians, New Spain meant death and destruction. The Spanish conquest had destroyed their cultures, and their leaders were killed in conflicts. Native Indian religions were threatened by the priests and monks, who demanded that Indians convert to Christianity. Disease and hardship killed many.

Spanish settlers began building the city of Morelia, Mexico, in 1541, ejecting the native people from their land.

By the end of the 1500s, there was actually a labor shortage in New Spain. So many Indians had died that the Spanish were forced to look elsewhere for workers. They turned to Africa. Before 1550, some 15,000 African slaves had been imported into New Spain. In later years, however, more and more would be brought in to provide a major portion of labor not just in New Spain, but in northern parts of America as well.

The Spanish Move North

The land north of Mexico seemed barren and poor in the eyes of the Spanish. Although the land was home to millions of Native Americans, there was no rich and powerful state like that of the Aztecs. Nevertheless, a number of Spanish adventurers hoping to find wealth, especially gold, entered this forbidding territory that would one day become the United States.

One of the first Spaniards to come to the northern regions was Juan Ponce de León. He arrived on the North American continent at what is now Florida, thinking he was still in the West Indies. He explored the coastline in 1512 and 1513, and was urged to return by Cortés in 1521.

> "Your greed for gold is blind. Your pride, your lust, your anger, your envy, your sloth, all blind. . . . You are in mortal sin."
>
> *Spanish monk Antón Montesino in a sermon to Spaniards, Santo Domingo, 1511*

Juan Ponce de León (c.1460–1521)

Juan Ponce de León went with Christopher Columbus on his second voyage to America in 1493. Between 1502 and 1504, Ponce de León took part in the conquest of the eastern part of Hispaniola. In 1508, he established a colony on Puerto Rico, where he discovered gold, and was made governor in 1509.

In Puerto Rico, Ponce de León heard a tale about an island called Bimini, where there was said to be a spring that restored youth to all who bathed in it. According to legend, he was seeking this spring ("the fountain of youth") when he came to Florida, although he was certainly more interested in gold than any magical waters.

On his second trip to Florida, in 1521, Ponce de León was wounded during an Indian attack. He was taken back to Cuba, where he soon died.

This Native American village in 17th-century Florida is like the settlements the first Spanish explorers would have seen. The Spanish soon began to build fortified settlements in the area for themselves.

In 1525, a Spanish expedition traveled up the coast as far north as what is now South Carolina. These travelers established a small settlement along the coast of present-day Georgia, with both African and Spanish inhabitants. This was the first Spanish attempt to create a town in North America. Within a few months, many settlers became ill and died. Some survivors returned to the Caribbean. It may be that some of the African slaves remained at the settlement.

Another remarkable expedition, led by Panfilo de Narvaez, began in Florida in 1527 and included some 300 men. The expedition traveled west along the coast, and finally reached what is now Texas. In November 1528, a huge storm struck the Spanish ships. The few survivors staggered ashore near present-day Galveston, Texas. There, local Indians seized the survivors and held them prisoner. Four eventually managed to escape, including an African slave named Estévan de Dorantes. Led by Álvar Núñez Cabeza de Vaca, the survivors walked to what is now New

Mexico, living among local Indian groups and convincing some that they were holy men. Turning south toward Mexico, they were rescued by Spanish slave hunters in 1536, almost nine years after their journey had begun.

When Cabeza de Vaca's story was published in Spain, more people became interested in exploring the northern regions of America. In 1539, the conquistador Hernando de Soto set out with nine ships and 600 men. They landed in

Hernando de Soto (c.1500–42)

Hernando de Soto was probably one of the most persistent searchers for gold in history. He was born in Barcarroto, Spain, and at the age of 19 sailed to America, where he soon earned a reputation for cruelty and courage.

In 1524 and 1526, De Soto took part in expeditions to Central America, and in 1532 he joined Francisco Pizarro in the conquest of Peru in South America. His share of the treasures stolen in Peru made him a rich man.

After a brief return to Spain, De Soto decided to look for wealth in the unknown areas of Florida. He persuaded the king of Spain to appoint him governor of Cuba and Florida. From his base in Havana, Cuba, De Soto and his party sailed for Florida. Their long journey took them far inland, where they faced hardship and the opposition of native peoples defending their territory. Whenever supplies and morale ran low, De Soto encouraged his men with the prospect of riches ahead.

De Soto was extremely cruel to the Indians. He forced them to hand over supplies, and tortured their chiefs in a vain effort to make them tell where gold was hidden. This cruelty forced the Indians to defend themselves. In a battle near Mobile Bay, on the Gulf of Mexico in present-day Alabama, some 70 Spaniards were killed and De Soto was wounded.

By the fall of 1541, the expedition had reached as far as present-day Oklahoma. After three years, De Soto had still not found gold. In the spring of 1542, he turned back and led his exhausted band of survivors southward. Near the junction of the Red River and the Mississippi River, De Soto fell ill and died.

Florida near Tampa Bay and went north into the Appalachian Mountains, searching for a rich civilization like that of the Aztecs. Turning westward, they roamed through what are now Alabama and Mississippi. In 1541, they became the first Europeans to come to the Mississippi River, which they crossed when traveling into present-day Arkansas.

The De Soto expedition used the usual brutal methods of the conquistadors in their meetings with native peoples. But a much worse result of this journey was the diseases brought by the Spanish to the people of the American Southeast. These diseases killed vast numbers of Indians, just as they had done farther south, and changed forever their societies and ways of life.

Hernando de Soto arrived at the Mississisppi River in 1541, having left Florida with a huge expedition two years before. De Soto was obsessed with the possibility of finding gold.

Search for the Seven Cities

In the early 1500s, New Spain was swept with rumors about fantastic civilizations and cities in unexplored areas. In 1540, Francisco Vásquez de Coronado, governor of New Galicia in Mexico, assembled about 300 Spaniards and 1,000 Indians to go north into the American Southwest in search of the fabled Seven Cities of Cíbola.

Entering what is now Arizona and New Mexico, they found instead poor pueblos in which the Zuñi people lived. Coronado quickly attacked and subdued them. Scouting parties then went as far north as the edge of the Grand Canyon, vainly looking for the Seven Cities.

New hope came when an Indian slave told of a rich land to the northeast. With 30 men and the slave as a guide, Coronado set out to find this land. After months, they had

settlers made their first base near present-day Albuquerque. Oñate proclaimed the royal colony of New Mexico and demanded that the native people pledge their loyalty to the king of Spain. Christian priests founded settlements, known as missions, and demanded labor from the Indian people whom they tried to convert to Christianity.

Oñate faced serious problems in New Mexico from the start. Some of his men wanted to mutiny against his rule and had to be subdued. In addition, the Indians would not cooperate, and a number of pueblos revolted in 1598 and 1599. Oñate's men brutally crushed these uprisings, killing men, women, and children in the process. Life for the Spanish was extremely dangerous for the next century, and some settlers returned to Mexico. A number remained, though, founding towns and isolated ranches on Apache and Navajo lands. Although the native people fought against their rule, the Spanish continued to push their claim to the American Southwest.

Santa Fe

Santa Fe, now the capital of the state of New Mexico, was founded in 1609. Today, the city is a living museum of Spanish and Indian history of the American Southwest.

The Spanish established many mission churches in the area. One of these churches still stands at the San Miguel Mission. San Miguel was built in 1636 and is the oldest church still in use in the United States. The Indians who built it for the Spanish used adobe, the sun-dried clay that was traditional in the area. Inside the church is the San José bell, which was made in Spain in the 1350s and brought to Santa Fe 300 years later.

The region's Indian heritage is equally visible today. On the 50-mile (80-km) drive southward toward the city of Albuquerque, the area is dotted with pueblos. These are now preserved on reservations, home to Native American groups who have lived in New Mexico for centuries.

The Spanish and Indian traditions exist side by side in a modern environment, as proof of the region's complex and diverse history.

5

The English Chesapeake Settlements

England was one of Spain's main rivals in Europe. The country had kept an interest in the Americas over the years. But in the mid-1500s, England was too weak to challenge Spanish power. Problems at home used up most of England's energies and resources. Nevertheless, English adventurers found ways of harassing the Spanish in the Americas, especially by raiding and stealing from ships carrying goods.

Explorers and Privateers

The journey of John Cabot had attempted to open a northwest passage to Asia but had failed. In 1576, almost 80 years after Cabot's voyage, the English attempted once again to find such a passageway. The explorer Martin Frobisher led an expedition to northern Canada, hoping to find a route to China. Like the Spanish, he was looking for gold, but the tons of "ore" he hauled back to England proved worthless.

By the 1570s, England and Spain were on a collision course toward war, and their rivalry was often played out in America. Spanish commerce was interrupted by English privateers. This was the name for adventurers who attacked Spanish outposts and shipping with the blessing of the English queen, Elizabeth I. The raids of men like Sir Francis Drake, Sir John Hawkins, and Sir Walter Raleigh became the stuff of legend. They represented a new class of Englishmen who were frustrated by the limitations of life in England and were eager to make their names and fortunes overseas. They did this first as privateers and later as founders of English settlements in North America.

The Spanish in the Americas took privateers very seriously. They had founded St. Augustine and other coastal settlements as bases and safe ports to protect their Caribbean trade. The English attacks posed a grave threat to this profitable activity.

The English-Spanish conflict in Europe eventually led to victory for the English. The mighty Spanish Armada was sent to attack England in 1588. The English defeated the Spanish warships in a huge naval battle, proving themselves to be a great sea power. At around this time, the English took the first steps toward building permanent settlements in America.

Early English Settlements

The first English settlements failed miserably. Communities founded in Newfoundland in the late 1570s and early 1580s were not successful. In 1585, Sir Walter Raleigh received permission from the English crown to start a settlement on Roanoke Island, off the coast of present-day North Carolina (see map on page 53). A small group sailed from England to establish the colony. In the group was the painter John White, whose beautiful drawings were the first realistic pictures of Native American people to be seen by Europeans.

Raleigh dreamed of a colony where whites, Indians, and Africans freed from Spanish slavery might live side by side.

In 1587, the English settlement on Roanoke Island held a baptism. Virginia Dare was the granddaughter of the colony's governor, artist John White. She was the first English child born in America.

The dream never came true. The early settlers depended on the native people for food. When relations between the two groups turned bad, the English had no way to feed themselves. Raleigh sent out more men in 1586 and 1587. After that, men were needed in Europe to fight the Spanish, and it was not until 1590 that men could be spared to return to Roanoke. When they landed, there was no one to be found.

What happened to the people of Roanoke colony has remained a mystery. But recent scientific discoveries have been made from looking at ancient trees in the area. It seems that a terrible drought from 1587 to 1589 may have caused the colony to perish.

The Chesapeake Settlements

The defeat of the Armada in 1588 proved that the English could dominate the Spanish in Europe. Perhaps they could do so in North America as well. Spain had made claims to huge areas of what is now the southern United States, but these were not defended. Most Spanish forces in the Americas were farther south, in Mexico, or in the Caribbean.

Roanoke had shown the English that settlements needed to be planned, and they needed money for supplies to keep going. In order to get money for starting new colonies, Englishmen began creating joint stock companies. People who bought shares in the companies were investing in settlement projects. The king, James I, heartily approved of the investment of private money, provided the crown received a share of the profits.

In 1606, the king granted a charter to a new joint stock company called the Virginia Company. This company was to start a colony in North America along the coast of present-day Virginia. In a grand gesture, James granted the company millions of acres of land. This was meaningless in reality, as it was land that he did not control. The Spanish claimed almost all the same land because of their early explorations. And the land was of course already inhabited by native peoples who had lived on it for centuries.

Some investors saw the Virginia Company project as a place for unemployed Englishmen, who could be shipped overseas to work in the new colony. Others thought that overseas settlements would be new markets where they could sell English wool cloth. Some investors just hoped for quick profits, thinking the settlers might find gold or silver.

In December 1606, 144 Englishmen in three ships set sail for North America. Four months later, 105 of them arrived at the mouth of the Chesapeake Bay off present-day Virginia. (The rest had died at sea.) They put ashore on a peninsula of the James River, some 60 miles (97 km) from the coast. They named their new settlement Jamestown after King James I.

Early European Settlements on the Northeastern Atlantic Coast

NEW ENGLAND

Hudson River

Connecticut River

Massachusetts Bay Colony

Boston

Plymouth

Cape Cod

Fort Nassau

NEW NETHERLAND

New Amsterdam (New York)

Delaware River

NEW SWEDEN

ATLANTIC OCEAN

VIRGINIA

James River

Jamestown

Chesapeake Bay

Roanoke River

Roanoke Island

miles 0 — 100

km 0 — 100

N

Settling on Indian Land

For the Englishmen arriving in Virginia, the new land was a wilderness. For the people who watched these strangers come ashore, the land had been home for generations. The Englishmen were settling on Indian land.

Powhatan was the head chief of a confederacy of Algonquin Indian tribes living in or near the Chesapeake region. He ruled over a group of chiefs who paid him a yearly tribute of deer hides as a sign of their loyalty. The men in Powhatan's chiefdom served as warriors. The women searched for food, cooked, planted crops, and raised children.

After the failed attempt to colonize Roanoke Island, Jamestown in Virginia was the first permanent English settlement on the eastern coast of North America. After 1620, settlements were built farther north, in New England (see chapter 6) and in what is now New York State (see chapter 8).

53

NEW ENGLAND

"Let this therefore assure you of our loves, and every year our friendly trade shall furnish you with corn; and now also, if you would come in friendly manner to see us, and not thus with guns and swords as to invade your foes."

Powhatan to John Smith in 1608

In 1614, John Smith, seen below, sailed along the eastern coast of North America. He made maps of the region and gave it the name "New England."

Powhatan's people were the first group in North America to come into extended contact with early English settlers. Their chief soon saw that he had to deal with these new inhabitants. Sometimes, the Englishmen were friendly, particularly when they needed food. At other times, however, they used their superior weapons to attack Powhatan's people, especially when they wanted to seize a piece of land.

Powhatan sometimes fought against these acts of violence, but he never organized any large-scale attempt to drive the white people out of the Chesapeake region. His probable reasons were simple: The settlers made better allies than enemies; they had powerful weapons; and they had goods to trade. Sailing ships arrived filled with things that the Indians wanted in exchange for corn. Powhatan especially wanted the English axes and swords that would give him power over other Indian groups.

Life in Jamestown

For the settlers, the early weeks and months in Jamestown were almost unbearable. Between May and September 1607, 50 of them died. After an early skirmish with the Indians, relations settled down and Powhatan kept the peace. However, the English quarreled among themselves and crops went unplanted. The Indians brought corn to trade with the survivors in the fall of 1607, but it wasn't enough. One of the group, Captain John Smith, was perhaps the most important leader the settlers had in these days, for his intelligence and persistence helped them survive during the early months of cold and hunger.

John Smith (c.1580–1631)

John Smith was born in Lincolnshire, England. In his later writings, he claimed that he fought in the war against the Turks in Hungary, that he was captured and sold into slavery, and that he escaped to Russia.

In 1605, Smith joined the expedition that was preparing to go to America to found the colony of Virginia. His strong leadership abilities led him to take charge of the Jamestown settlement, and he issued the famous order, "He who will not work shall not eat." Smith also encouraged good relations with the native people. He realized that if they were to survive, the settlers would have to trade with and learn from the Indians.

Smith returned to England and wrote several books about North America. While a number of historians question the truth of some of Smith's accounts, there is no doubt that many of his writings provided much information about the life of the early settlers of Jamestown.

There were only 38 colonists still alive in January 1608 when 200 new settlers arrived from England. The Virginia Company was committed to sending new settlers to the Chesapeake colony, but many of the new arrivals also died, and the winter of 1609–10 was one of great hardship and starvation. By 1610, a total of 500 settlers had been sent from England; about 440 had died.

Part of the problem was that many of the settlers had never done physical work. Fishing and hunting for food were at first neglected, and many settlers refused to farm. There is evidence that the early Jamestown years were also a time of serious drought. Shortage of food and good drinking water probably caused many deaths. It would also have contributed to problems betwen the white settlers and the Indians.

Powhatan died in 1618. His brother Opechancaneough became head chief. Unlike Powhatan, his brother had a fierce dislike of the English. In 1622, he organized an all-out attack on their settlements. The settlers in return started a campaign to exterminate the native population once and for all. The uneasy truce maintained in the time of Powhatan

"So lamentable was our scarcity that we were constrained to eat dogs, cats, rats, snakes, toadstools, horsehides, and what not. . . ."

English settler describing winter of 1609 in Jamestown

Pocahontas (c.1595-1617)

One of the most enduring stories of American history is about Pocahontas, the daughter of Powhatan.

Ætatis suæ 21. A. 1616.

According to John Smith's later writings, Pocahontas saved his life after he had been captured by Powhatan's warriors and was about to be killed. When Pocahontas pleaded with her father to spare him, Powhatan agreed, and Smith was allowed to go free. This may or may not have taken place, but Pocahontas did play an important part in keeping the peace between her people and the early Jamestown settlers. She often brought food to the starving settlers in their early years, and they were fond of her.

However, when relations between Powhatan and the settlers had become strained, Pocahontas was taken hostage by Captain Samuel Argall, who took her to Jamestown. Argall hoped to use Pocahontas to make a peace settlement with Powhatan's people.

Pocahontas was treated with respect by the citizens of Jamestown. While there, she became a Christian and took the name Rebecca. She also met John Rolfe, a young widower who was the first colonist to grow tobacco as a crop. In 1614, Rolfe requested permission to marry Pocahontas. Powhatan was pleased by the proposal because it created an alliance with the English. Pocahontas and Rolfe were married on April 5, 1614, in the Anglican church at Jamestown.

In 1616, the Rolfes sailed to England for a visit. The English were fascinated with Pocahontas. She was received by King James I at his palace and was a guest of the Bishop of London. The Rolfes prepared to return to Virginia, but before they sailed Pocahontas caught smallpox. She died in March 1617 in Gravesend, England.

came to a sudden end. Warfare and white men's diseases took their terrible toll among Powhatan's people, and the English became more and more powerful as they took over the land.

A Royal Colony

The clash with the Indians in 1622 proved to be a turning point. Nearly 350 settlers were killed in this bloody conflict, about a third of the white population. Up until that point, the colonists had thought the Native Americans were necessary for their survival. After that date, they believed that their survival would not be possible unless the original inhabitants were killed.

Another change resulting from the events of 1622 was a difference in the way the colony was run. The war with the Indians had shocked the government in England, and an investigation was made. As a result of this inquiry, King James I took away the charter of the Virginia Company and made Virginia into a royal colony. From then on, the settlement was ruled by the king through a governor, not by the private investors of the Virginia Company.

The settlement of Jamestown has been recreated at its original site, complete with people in costume performing the everyday activities of the colonists.

Barrels of dried tobacco leaves being rolled to ships bound for England. By 1618, the colonists were shipping 20,000 pounds (9,000 kg) of tobacco to England. By 1700, that amount had increased to 17,500 tons (15,870 metric tons) a year from Virginia and Maryland combined.

Even before it became a royal colony, the settlement had begun to create its own institutions of government. The settlers established a House of Burgesses, which was a kind of parliament. The House of Burgesses proposed laws that went into effect if the Virginia Company approved them. Under royal rule, the Burgesses were allowed to remain, but their laws now had to be approved by the governor.

By 1624, the population of Virginia was still only about 1,200. Most of the thousands who had migrated there were now dead, but settlers still came. The English were in North America for good.

Tobacco Plantations

Almost by accident, the early settlers discovered a crop that was to make them a lot of money: tobacco. Tobacco already grew wild in the Americas. Native Americans rolled tobacco leaves, lit them, and inhaled the smoke. Europeans had never seen such a thing before, but they soon started doing it themselves.

In 1612, the colonist John Rolfe planted some West Indian tobacco seeds. The plant did well in the soil of Virginia, and five years later, the first commercial shipment of Virginia tobacco left for England. It sold extremely well. The colonists of Virginia were on their way to becoming tobacco planters.

Soon, large expanses of wilderness in the Chesapeake region were interrupted here and there by tobacco farms. A typical tobacco farm had about five to ten acres (2–4 ha) under cultivation. As the soil became poor from too much planting, farmers would simply move to new parts of their land where the soil was fresh. A typical family farm consisted of 150 to 200 acres (60–80 ha), much of it forest. But often just five to ten acres were under cultivation at one time.

> "All our riches for the present do consist in tobacco."
>
> *A Chesapeake planter in 1630*

The New Labor Force

Tobacco required hard work and much tending. A system called indentured servitude developed to fill the need for tobacco workers. The system allowed a poor worker from Europe to come to the colonies in return for a certain period of unpaid labor. The worker would sign a contract agreeing to work without pay, usually for a period of four to seven years. In return, the worker's passage by ship to America would be paid.

On the ship's arrival in America, the captain would sell the indenture contract. Contracts were usually sold to a tobacco planter, sometimes for twice the value of the passage. The indenture was then owned by the tobacco planter, who provided food, clothing, and shelter in exchange for work. However an employer could, if he wished, sell the contract on to someone else. In a way indentured servants were like slaves, except that after the indenture period was finished, the servant was free.

For the planters, buying an indenture was a good deal because they got a period of guaranteed free labor. The average indentured servant was a male between the ages of 15 and 25 who did farm work. Planters were also eager

"But I have nothing at all – no, not a shirt to my back but two rags. . . . I have not a penny, not a penny worth, to help me either to spice or sugar or strong waters."

Richard Frehorne, indentured servant in Virginia, writing to his parents in England in 1623

to buy the contracts of skilled men, such as blacksmiths and carpenters. Only one in four indentured servants was a woman. Female servants were sometimes used in the fields, but more often they were given household duties.

Indentured servitude was long and hard, but it offered the chance of a new life. In England, there was little hope for poor people to acquire their own property. As indentured servants in America, they were promised a piece of land when they finished their service. For many, the risk was worth taking.

Punishments, even for petty crimes, could involve having years added to an indenture contract. One servant in early America had six years added to his indenture for killing a pig that did not belong to him. The death rate was high in early Chesapeake society, and many indentured servants never lived long enough to see their dream of freedom and a farm of their own come true. Perhaps as many as half died before they were freed.

Workers from Africa

In 1619, the first Africans were brought to the Chesapeake settlements. Not all Africans in the early settlements were slaves. In fact, the colonies of Virginia and Maryland did not even have laws about slavery until after 1660. Some Africans may have been household slaves, as were some Indians. But slavery in this early period was not necessarily passed from one generation to the next. Up until 1660, there were fewer than 1,000 black slaves in Virginia and Maryland. In any case, slaves were too expensive for most planters. An indentured servant was a much better investment, and usually preferred.

All this was to change in later years. In the late 1600s, a labor shortage developed in England. As a result, wages went up and life improved for some poorer people. Indentured servitude in America became less attractive. Besides this, English immigrants now had other places to go in the colonies, such as Pennsylvania. As fewer indentured servants arrived, more African laborers were brought to work on the tobacco plantations. By 1700, indentured servants in Virginia had been replaced by slaves. The role of black people became clearer. Children born to slaves now became slaves themselves. Slavery became an accepted system with laws and regulations.

The House of Burgesses

In the early 1600s, English settlers made the first steps toward elected assemblies for governing themselves in the colonies. The House of Burgesses first met in 1619, in a Jamestown church. Its 22 members were delegates, which meant they had been elected by other English settlers to represent their views when decisions were being made. Each of 11 districts in the area sent two delegates to represent them in the House. Exactly who could vote for delegates in these early days is not certain, but it is likely that the voters were all male, all white, and all heads of households.

Within a week of their first meeting, the Burgesses passed many laws about behavior, distribution and use of land, and education of Indian children. The House of Burgesses did not have the full powers of an independent legislature. Their laws could be vetoed by the Virginia Company, and later by the British governor. But a pattern had been laid, and this kind of representative government would carry on through the colonial period and into the era of American independence.

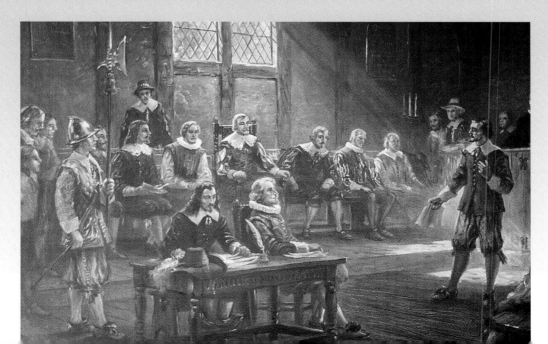

6

English Settlements in New England

Not every English settler in America came in search of riches or as an indentured servant. Many early English settlers came to New England in search of religious freedom. They also wanted the opportunity to live without interference from an all-powerful government.

The Puritans in England

In the early 1500s, the Catholic Church was splitting apart in many countries of Europe. This period was called the Reformation. It resulted in Christianity being divided between Roman Catholicism and various Protestant groups. Although Protestants were still Christians, they did not accept the Catholic pope as their religious leader.

In the 1530s, King Henry VIII of England broke away from the Roman Catholic Church and established the Church of England, a Protestant church. The king seized the Catholic Church's property in England: its monasteries, buildings, and lands. As the head of the new Church of England, the king not only had complete power over religious life, but now he had new sources of wealth.

Henry VIII was not interested in making big changes to religious beliefs and practices. But there was a group within the new Church of England who wanted to make major changes. They wanted to purify, or reform, the Church.

This group, known as the Puritans, believed that their faith should be based on the Bible, and only the Bible. They didn't want to rely on priests and bishops, and thought that Catholic rituals didn't belong in the Protestant faiths. They had strict religious principles and frowned on "frivolous" pursuits in life such as dancing or drinking liquor.

The Puritans believed they were God's elect people, and as such should rule over the "damned," meaning everyone else. By the late 1500s and early 1600s, they had become a threat to the English crown's control. They were challenging royal authority on all levels of life. King James I, who was crowned in 1603, resisted the Puritans. Many of them began to doubt they could gain the power they wanted. One group of Puritans, known as Separatists, wanted to pull out of the Church of England altogether. They decided to leave England and make a society elsewhere that they believed would be built on the word of God.

Puritan Migrations to North America

One of the first groups of Separatists to leave England moved to a village in Holland in 1608. The Dutch were more tolerant toward different religious groups. But to many of the Separatist Puritans, they seemed too tolerant. Fearing that their children would lost their "pure" faith, the Puritans decided to move again. This time they set their sights on America.

This Separatist group, who came to be known as "the Pilgrims," got permission from the Virginia Company to settle on its lands. To pay for their journey, the Pilgrims formed a joint stock company with a group of investors in London. The settlers agreed to share with their investors any profits they made in the first seven years.

In September 1620, 101 people (35 of whom were Separatists) boarded their ship, the *Mayflower*, and headed west across the Atlantic toward Virginia. After a journey of 11 weeks, they sighted land off what is now the coast of Cape Cod, Massachusetts (see map on page 53).

The travelers knew that they were in the wrong place and that they had no authority to land there. (Some historians believe that they intentionally went farther north than they were supposed to.) But the November weather was fierce, and the journey across the ocean had been dreadful. They decided to stay where they were. Before going ashore, the expedition leaders drew up the Mayflower Compact, a pact under which they agreed to govern themselves, and to enact and obey any laws necessary for the well-being and survival of the group. All the men on the ship, including those who were not Pilgrims, signed the Mayflower Compact.

In December, the travelers went ashore and named their settlement Plymouth. The land they chose to settle on had already been cleared by its original inhabitants. It was farmland belonging to the native village of Patuxet. Most of Patuxet's inhabitants had died from disease about three years before the English settlers arrived. The epidemic was probably spread by John Smith's expedition from Virginia, when he had come north to explore the region.

Still aboard ship, the Pilgrims and their fellow travelers sign an agreement. The Mayflower Compact, as it was called, set out a plan for government in the new colony and promised "just and equal laws."

The settlers found the environment extremely hostile that first winter. They survived however they could, which included taking supplies from Indian houses, foodstores, and even graves. Within three months of going ashore, about half of the settlers had died. Their condition was not helped by the severity of the winter, which was unusually cold and damp. Among those who died in the first few months was John Carver, who had acted as governor of the colony. In 1621, the colonists elected William Bradford, another leading Pilgrim, as their new governor. Bradford went on to govern the Plymouth colony for many years. He always tried to maintain good relations with the Native Americans on whose land the colonists had settled.

The Pilgrims might not have survived without the help of Indians during the spring of 1621. The Plymouth settlement had been founded on the homeland of the Wampanoag. Their chief, Massasoit, was friendly toward the newcomers. He probably had no other choice, because they had firearms that could have been used against his people. Besides this, the Wampanoag people were still weakened and reduced in numbers by disease.

The Pilgrims come ashore to a harsh and wintry landscape in 1620. By the time they arrived, most of them were sick, and some travelers had died on the journey from England.

The Wampanoag showed the new settlers how to plant corn, where and how to fish, and how to store food for the coming winter. Later that year, in November 1621, the Pilgrims held a feast of thanksgiving at which Massasoit and some of his warriors were guests.

That same month, 36 new settlers arrived from England. Times were still hard, but crops were planted and a handful of small, sturdy buildings had been constructed. The settlement was secured.

Squanto teaches survival skills to white settlers in the Plymouth colony.

Squanto (15?–1622)

One of the people most important to the Pilgrims' survival was a Patuxet man named Tisquantum, or Squanto. The date of Squanto's birth is not known.

He was taken to England around 1605, and nine years later brought back to North America by John Smith. Shortly afterward, he was kidnapped by an English ship's captain and sold into slavery in Spain. Squanto eventually escaped and returned to England. From there he was taken back to New England in 1619.

Upon his return, he found that his entire village had died of smallpox. Squanto went to live among the Wampanoag nearby. Because he could speak English, Governor William Bradford asked him to be a go-between for the English settlers and the Indians. Together with other Wampanoag people, Squanto taught the settlers how to survive by growing and catching food, and also acted as their guide and interpreter.

Squanto died in 1622 while guiding an expedition to Cape Cod.

Peace with the white settlers lasted through Massasoit's lifetime. But as the settlers took more and more Wampanoag lands over the years, tension grew.

The Massachusetts Bay Colony

Meanwhile in England, the Puritans had gained a strong influence in Parliament. Relations between the English king, now Charles I, and Parliament got steadily worse. When the king dissolved Parliament in 1629, many Puritans decided it was time to leave the country for good.

A group of wealthy Puritans, including the lawyer John Winthrop, formed the Massachusetts Bay Company in 1629. They were given a royal charter to settle an area in North America, which is now northern New England (see map on page 53). The company was also given a right that hadn't been granted to others: It would have its own government in America, rather than London. This gave the Massachusetts Bay Company a great amount of control, free of interference from investors and the crown.

In 1630, 11 ships carrying more than 700 people (about half of them Puritans) sailed for North America. Before leaving England the emigrants had elected John Winthrop as their governor. Winthrop believed the Puritans in his group had entered a "covenant with God." Their aim, he told them, was to build a new society according to God's plan and to resist the temptations of the devil. Unlike the Pilgrims, who separated themselves from the Church of England, these new settlers wanted to establish a model for other Christians in their Church to follow.

John Winthrop (1588–1649)

John Winthrop, a Puritan born in Suffolk, England, was a rich landowner and lawyer. His family had acquired its property when Henry VIII seized land from the Catholics.

Winthrop was unhappy with conditions for Puritans in England, and joined a group emigrating to America. He became an officer of the Massachussets Bay Company and was chosen as governor of their new colony. The rest of his life was devoted to governing the Massachusetts Bay Colony. Winthrop's _Journal_, also called _The History of New England_, is a valuable historical record of life in the early settlements in America.

Winthrop had 16 children. His son, John, became governor of Connecticut, as did his grandson.

John Winthrop and other Puritan settlers come ashore in Massachusetts in 1630. With Winthrop as governor, Massachusetts became the first self-governing colony in America.

The Puritans arrived in Massachusetts and founded a colony at Charlestown. Lack of water there caused them to move to the nearby peninsula of Shawmut. Eventually, they settled on the site that became the city of Boston (see map on page 53). The settlers did not have anything to do with the Separatists who lived in Plymouth. Instead, they built their own community, planting crops to store for the next winter. At first, they met few Indians in their part of New England. Epidemics of disease had killed most of them before the Massachusetts Bay Colony was established.

The first months were very hard on the settlers in Massachusetts Bay Colony. More than 200 died in the first year, and others decided to return to England on the first available ship. Still, thousands of others arrived to take their place between 1630 and 1640. Most of them, although not all, were Puritans.

In Chesapeake Bay, most immigrants had been indentured servants, and were mainly men. But it was different in New England, where more farmers and tradesmen arrived. This is probably because whole Puritan villages would uproot themselves and emigrate together from England. This meant also that there was a balance of men, women, and children.

"We shall be as a city upon a hill, the eyes of all people are upon us."

John Winthrop, 1630

68

In the 1600s, the Massachusetts Bay Colony founded more than 130 towns, most of them along rivers and some as far distant as present-day New Hampshire, Connecticut, and Rhode Island. Because the Puritans dominated these communities, each town had a church and a pastor whose role it was to ensure that members of the community followed God's will. Even when the Puritans were in a minority, they still had control. Under the Colony's charter, power was given only to men who were householders and members of the church.

Puritans in Indian Land

The Puritans' view of themselves as God's chosen people did not spell good news for the native peoples. Early in their settlement, some Puritans questioned whether they had the right to take land from people who had been there before them. In 1633, they thought they had an answer. That year, thousands of Indians were wiped out by smallpox. John Winthrop decided this catastrophe was a sign from God for the white man to take control of the land. Why would God have reduced the number of Indians, he asked, if not to make room for the Puritans?

"Oh New England, New England, how much I am bound to the Lord for granting me so great mercy as to tread on thy grounds."

Edward Trelawney writing to his brother in England in1635

As settlers moved outward from Massachusetts Bay, some founded communities that rejected Massachusetts rule. In the 1630s, the Reverend Thomas Hooker brought his congregation to settle in what is now Connecticut. The area became a separate colony with its own governing body.

69

Indian medicines and herbs offered no cure to the terrible epidemics that swept through New England. Most native people along the New England coast in the 1620s died from European diseases.

Indians, according to the Puritans, were not inferior; they were "sinners," and sinners needed to be converted to Christianity. In the 1640s, the Massachusetts Bay Colony passed laws to stop Native Americans from practicing their own religions. At times, the Puritans used violence against the Indians, and demanded that they follow English customs.

A Puritan minister translated the Bible into Algonquian, and a number of "mission towns," or "praying towns," were established for Native Americans. Only a small number of Indians actually became Christians or joined the mission communities. But as diseases killed many over the years, the native population became less of a threat to the white settlers of the Massachusetts Bay Colony.

Puritan Expansion

The Puritan colonization of New England began with little resistance from Indians. Their numbers had been reduced by epidemics of disease, the first occurring two years before the arrival of the Puritans, and a second in 1633 to 1634. Both epidemics drastically cut the Indian population.

Puritan expansion farther south, however, met with resistance. The most serious event was the Pequot War in 1637 in Connecticut. The Pequot people controlled the fur trade in the Connecticut River valley, and they resisted the English settlers taking over their land. They were crushed in a bloody conflict when Puritans attacked a Pequot village and killed more than 500 men, women, and children. Many survivors were taken as slaves or given over to pro-English Indian groups as captives. Puritan expansion could then go on without interference.

French Explorers and Traders

Like Spain and England, France sent explorers and settlers to America and claimed huge areas of land as its own. The Spanish had conquered the vast lands of the south. The English hovered in small coastal settlements in the Chesapeake and New England. And France explored deep into the North American continent, starting in what is now Canada.

Jacques Cartier's Expeditions

In 1534, the navigator Jacques Cartier sailed across the Atlantic at the command of King Francis I of France, who wanted to find wealth and a northwestern passage to Asia. Cartier explored the western coast of Newfoundland before arriving at what is now Prince Edward Island. He then explored the coast of New Brunswick and landed on the Gaspé Peninsula, which is now part of the province of Quebec.

For some time, the English had been sending fishing boats to the waters off northeastern Canada. Before Cartier's exploration, the region had been considered too cold for anything else. But Cartier discovered that the climates of New Brunswick and the Gaspé were fairly warm, and the land seemed good enough for farming.

In 1535, Cartier returned to North America for another two years of exploration. He sailed up the St. Lawrence River as far as the present-day city of Quebec. Cartier left some of his men by the river to set up winter quarters, and went on to the Indian village of Hochelaga, where the city

Jacques Cartier (above) made three expeditions to what is now Canada, years before the English settled on the North American continent. But no permanent French colonies emerged in Canada until the 1600s.

of Montreal now stands. On his return, he explored the Cabot Strait and confirmed that Newfoundland was an island.

Cartier's third trip to North America, in 1541, was paid for by a French nobleman, Jean Francois de Roberval. De Roberval was interested in establishing a colony, and he and Cartier traveled to Canada with ten ships, about 400 soldiers, 300 sailors, and a few women.

The expedition arrived in the St. Lawrence valley. The travelers built a fortified settlement on Native American lands. The Indians had already been in conflict with Cartier on his two earlier journeys, and the settlement only made relations worse.

The French soon began to suffer from scurvy, a painful and weakening illness caused by lack of fresh food. This, and frequent attacks by native inhabitants, caused heavy casualties among the French. They gave up the attempt to colonize the St. Lawrence valley, and Cartier's search for riches had also failed. Despite this, French claims to the whole of northeastern Canada were based on Cartier's explorations. This area became known as New France.

The Huguenots

The next French attempt at colonization was in present-day South Carolina, in 1562, when some Huguenots (French Protestants) briefly established a community there. In 1564, they tried again, near what is now Jacksonville, Florida. A year later, all the settlers were massacred by the Spanish, and the settlement was burned to the ground. Since France then became involved in a civil war between Huguenots and Catholics, it would not try to colonize again until the 1600s.

Early Fur-Trading Settlements

The French never found gold, but they realized that there was another source of wealth in North America. That source was fur. During the late 1500s, hats made from beaver fur became very popular all over Europe. Beavers were almost extinct in Europe, but fishermen along the coast of northern New England and Newfoundland found that they could trade with the native peoples for fur, including beaver. In exchange, the Europeans gave the Indians knives, axes, cloth, and glass beads. The beads were valued by the Indians, for whom they may have had some sacred meaning.

Between 1598 and 1604, the French founded a number of fur-trading outposts along the coast of Nova Scotia. The French fur traders understood a simple fact: If they were to get fur, they needed to establish good, businesslike relations

Coureurs de Bois

This French term, meaning "wood runners," referred to the early fur traders in New France. They ignored regulations and went into the Canadian wilderness to trade with the native peoples. They would live for months at a time with Indian trappers, who traded their skills and furs for European tools, weapons, blankets, and liquor.

At one time, a large number of the white men in New France were coureurs de bois. They contributed to exploration and to the growth of the fur trade, but they caused problems for the government of the French colony. They also had an effect on the societies they traded with, for Native Americans became more dependent on their goods.

> "They come like foxes, they attack like lions, they disappear like birds."
>
> *French priest describing attack by Iroquois in 1648*

with the Native Americans. They realized that it was in their own interest to deal fairly with those peoples who were willing to trade with them.

Alliance with the Huron

One Frenchman who understood this quite well was Samuel de Champlain. In 1608, Champlain founded a settlement along the St. Lawrence River. This site later became Quebec, the capital of a great colony and the center of New France.

Χ To guarantee the safety of the new settlement, Champlain made an agreement with the Huron people. In exchange for furs, Champlain traded European goods. He formed a pact with the Huron against the powerful Iroquois confederacy to the south, which the French considered a threat to their fur trade. The Iroquois had reason to be hostile to the French. In 1609, Champlain had attacked and defeated them near Crown Point, New York.

The explorer Samuel de Champlain, backed by Algonquin allies, fires on a group of Iroquois Indians in 1609.

New France as a Settlement

Although the fur trade was a success, New France never became a thriving colony of settlers. French farmers and workers did not feel the need to leave their country. Unlike the poor in England, they could own land and did not suffer food shortages. And New France never seemed like an attractive destination, partly due to its frigid winters.

Χ The Protestant Huguenots might have considered leaving their country, like the English Puritans, to seek religious freedom. However, they were

Samuel de Champlain (1567–1635)

Samuel de Champlain was born in Brouage, France. His father was a sea captain, and Samuel was trained in seamanship, navigation, and map-making. As a young navigator, Champlain commanded a two-year voyage to the West Indies and Mexico. He brought back information about the Spanish in Central America, and was granted a noble title by King Henry IV of France.

In 1603, Champlain joined an expedition to find good sites for settlement and trading in Canada. He explored the coast of Maine and made the first detailed charts of the region. He also helped establish an early settlement in Nova Scotia, which was abandoned after three years when it lost the support of the French government.

On an expedition in 1609, Champlain came to the lake that now bears his name. He explored the Great Lakes region in 1615, and eventually settled down to manage Quebec. He visited France often to seek help on the colony's behalf. In 1629, the British took over Quebec and Champlain was taken to England as a prisoner. He was released in 1632, and the colony was returned to French control. Champlain went back to Quebec as governor in 1633 and died there in 1635. Because of his many important acts, Champlain has been called "the Father of New France."

actually prevented from moving to New France. The French government feared that Huguenots in an overseas colony could be a threat to the crown. They might be able to raise an army in Canada and use it to overthrow the French king. In addition, the French government wanted to keep the peasant population in France. It needed the manpower for its rivalries with England and Spain.

For all these reasons, the French population of New France was only a little over 15,000 by the late 1600s. This was small compared to the English colonies, which by that time had more than 100,000 white residents. Nonetheless, the French continued to have an active interest in exploring the farther reaches of the North American continent. They pushed inland looking for new sources of fur, all the while claiming the lands they explored for the French crown.

French Exploration Continues

In 1671, Jacques Marquette, a French priest, founded a mission on the shore of the Straits of Mackinac between Lake Michigan and Lake Huron. A fur trader and explorer named Louis Jolliet arrived at the mission the following year. The governor of New France had asked him to find a great river described by Indians, and Marquette was to go with Jolliet on the expedition. In May 1673, they left with five other men, traveling in bark canoes.

They eventually came to the Mississippi River in present-day Wisconsin, and were among the first Europeans to see its

Marquette (standing, second from right) and Jolliet (seated, behind Marquette) explore the Mississippi River.

upper portion. For a month, the expedition traveled down the river until they reached the mouth of the Arkansas River. They learned that the Mississippi flowed into the Gulf of Mexico but that to reach the Gulf, they would have to pass through Spanish territory. They decided to turn back. In less than five months, Marquette and Jolliet had traveled more than 2,500 miles (4,000 km).

Eight years later, in 1681, the fur trader René Robert Cavelier, Sieur de La Salle, went down the Mississippi River. He arrived at the river's mouth on the Gulf of Mexico in 1682. La Salle claimed the entire Mississippi River valley and the Great Lakes region for France. He named this vast area Louisiana, in honor of the French king, Louis XIV.

French explorers traveled huge distances in their explorations of the northern parts of North America. And settlements were founded, even though the population was small compared to the English colonies farther south.

> "The life I am leading has no other attraction for me other than that of honor; and the more danger and difficulty there is in undertakings of this sort, the more worthy of honour I think they are."
>
> *Sieur de La Salle.*

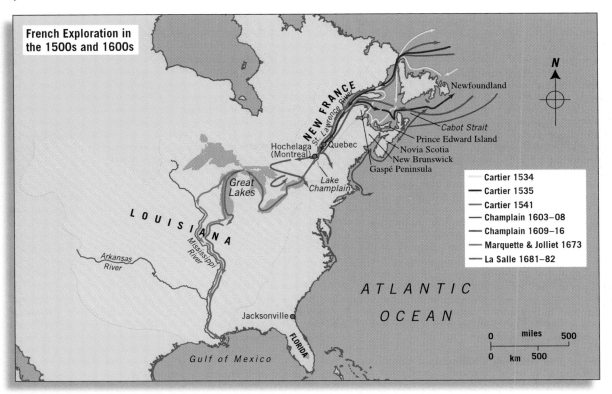

French Exploration in the 1500s and 1600s

—	Cartier 1534
—	Cartier 1535
—	Cartier 1541
—	Champlain 1603–08
—	Champlain 1609–16
—	Marquette & Jolliet 1673
—	La Salle 1681–82

"Their soul is a soil which is naturally good, but loaded down with all the evils that a land abandoned since the birth of the world can produce. . . . They are very much attached to each other, and agree admirably. You do not see any disputes . . . or reproaches among them."

Paul Le Jeune, a French priest, about Native Americans, 1634

The French Priests

In spite of their low numbers, the French kept a strong religious presence in North America. From the early 1600s, French priests attempted to spread Catholicism among the Native Americans. They worked especially with the Huron, with whom there was a flourishing fur trade.

Generally, French priests were not as harsh toward the native people as were the Spanish and English. Unlike Spanish priests, the French lived in Indian villages. Most important, they did not remove people or use them for forced labor. French priests tried to use native values and beliefs to help convert people to Christianity. For example, they made the story of Jesus's birth sound more like an Indian folktale. They told how he had been born in a piece of broken bark and had been wrapped in a robe made of rabbit skin.

In the early years of New France, however, few Indians converted to Christianity. They preferred their own religious beliefs and ways of looking at the universe.

The French in Canada

French people were to play an important part in the history of North America. Because of their settlement in Canada and exploration of the Great Lakes and Mississippi regions, the French made a claim to a significant piece of the continent. The British often claimed the very same territories. Over time, these rivals would see their centuries of European conflict spill into North America. One day they would battle it out for control of the entire continent.

Long after those conflicts have ended, however, French culture lives on in Canada. Modern Canada is a bilingual country: Both English and French are its official languages. In the province of Quebec, where most people speak French, there has been a political movement to separate from Canada and become an independent nation. Although the movement to "free Quebec" has not succeeded in its goal, it came close in a recent vote on the question of independence.

Early Dutch Settlements

The Dutch Republic (also called the Netherlands, or Holland) was a great power in Europe during the 1600s. The Netherlands were under Spanish control, but in 1588 the Dutch-speaking northern provinces became independent. They were then known as the Dutch Republic. The southern provinces of the Netherlands (now Belgium and Luxembourg) remained under Spanish control until 1713.

The Dutch Republic occupied a very small area of land compared with France, England, or Spain. But what they lacked in territory the Dutch people made up in their role as a great seafaring nation. After its independence, the Dutch Republic built a trading empire stretching from Brazil to West Africa to Indonesia. North America was quite a small part of this great commercial empire, but even so, the Dutch played a major role in its settlement.

Dutch Commercial Exploration

Dutch exploration was paid for by private companies hoping to make money. In 1609, the Dutch East India Company sent an Englishman, Henry Hudson, to look for a passage to Asia. They were hoping to expand their trade with other countries.

Hudson first tried to find a northeast passage through the Arctic north of Europe and Russia. When that failed, he changed direction and attempted to find a northwest passage through America. Hudson sailed along the northeastern coast and traveled up the river that now carries his name: the great Hudson River in southeastern New York, which runs into the Atlantic at New York City.

Henry Hudson (c.1575–1611)

Henry Hudson was an explorer who worked for the Dutch and English. Although he did not succeed in his search for a passage through America to the East, his four voyages added greatly to European knowledge about the Arctic region and North America.

In 1607, Hudson made the first of two voyages for the English Muscovy Company. He sailed to Greenland and looked for a passage through the heavy ice surrounding the island of Spitsbergen. His second voyage, in 1608, followed the same route. This time, he traveled farther eastward along the Russian Arctic border, but he was forced by ice and cold to turn back.

The Dutch interest in the New York region came largely from Hudson's third voyage, during 1609. In 1610, a group of English adventurers backed his fourth voyage. Hudson sailed deep into northern Canada, entering the bay that now bears his name. His ship, the *Discovery*, was caught in ice much of the winter. Angry at the hardship they faced, most of the crew mutinied. In June 1611, Hudson, his son, and seven other sailors were forced into a small boat by the mutineers and abandoned in Hudson Bay to die in the cold.

Hudson on his voyage of 1609.

The Dutch soon saw the opportunity to trade for fur in the regions Hudson had visited. As early as 1611, they were trading with the Indians in the Hudson valley (see map on page 53). In 1614, they built Fort Nassau, near present-day Albany, New York. About that time, the Dutch West India Company was formed and given exclusive rights by the Dutch government to trade in the Western Hemisphere.

Besides trading for fur, the Dutch wanted to compete with the Spanish, who controlled trade between the West Indies and Europe. To do this, the Dutch built stations in northeastern America. These could be used for supplying and repairing ships traveling across the Atlantic.

In 1624, the West India Company built forts along the Hudson River in New York, and along the Delaware and Connecticut Rivers. In 1626, Peter Minuit of the West India Company bought the island of Manhattan from the Canarsee people with goods valued at the cost of a few beaver pelts. Minuit's deal with the Canarsees was more of a theft than a purchase. Apart from anything else, the island of Manhattan was actually inhabited by the Weckquaesgeeks, while the Canarsees lived at nearby Brooklyn.

The settlement of New Amsterdam was founded on the southern tip of Manhattan. Other settlements were built in the area, and together these Dutch communities were known as New Netherland. (See map on page 53.)

Peter Minuit buys Manhattan for the Dutch West India Company in 1626. He went on to found the town of New Amsterdam on the island. Minuit returned to Europe in 1631 and then came back to America a few years later to found another colony, that of New Sweden.

81

"The country here is generally like Germany. The land is good, and fruitful in everything which supplies human needs. . . . The people and Indians here in this country are like Dutchmen in body and stature . . . . [The Indians'] money consists of certain little bones, made of shells or cockles, which are found on the seabeach."

Johannes
Megapolensis,
Dutch minister,
in a letter, 1644

New Amsterdam was governed by the West India Company. The whole colony was on land that was also claimed by the English. However, the English were in conflict with France and Spain in Europe, and they did not challenge the Dutch settlements for the time being.

New Netherland never attracted as many immigrants as did New England and the Chesapeake settlements. The Dutch economy was prosperous and provided enough jobs for seamen and farm workers, so they stayed at home.

The Dutch West India Company, however, tried to attract rich people to come and live in New Netherland. It offered them patroonships, which were grants of land along the Hudson River. These tracts of land were up to 18 miles (29 km) in length. In return the new proprietor, or patroon, would agree to bring 50 families to the colony within four years. But most poor European immigrants hoped for their own land, and so the patroonships failed to attract many settlers. Only one patroon, a wealthy diamond merchant named Kiliaen Van Rensselaer, attracted enough settlers to his estate to keep his land grant.

New Netherland's population as a whole remained low. By the 1640s, only about 1,500 people lived there, most of them in New Amsterdam.

New Amsterdam's Society

The population of New Amsterdam was very mixed. Only about half the settlers were Dutch. The rest were Germans, French, Scandinavians, and Africans (both enslaved and free). Some settlers had moved there from other colonies for religious reasons, especially from the less tolerant region of New England. Others were sailors and merchants in the West Indian trade who had come to New Amsterdam and decided to stay.

Some Dutch settlers did not like this mix of nationalities. In the mid-1640s, one resident told a visitor that 18 different languages could be heard spoken in New Amsterdam. Another wrote to the Netherlands to complain that the town was filling up with people who did not believe in God, and other "servants of the Devil."

The governor of New Netherland from 1646 to 1664 was Peter Stuyvesant, an official of the Dutch West India Company. He was a stern and authoritarian ruler. As a member of the Dutch Reformed Church and a strict Protestant, Stuyvesant wanted everyone to conform to the Dutch church. It was a losing battle, and the Company realized this. They ordered Stuyvesant to allow people to have their own religious beliefs.

Peter Stuyvesant (c.1610–72)

Peter Stuyvesant was the last Dutch ruler of New Netherland. He was a commanding but very unpopular figure in the history of Dutch colonial rule in America.

Stuyvesant was born in Holland, the son of a Calvinist minister. He entered military service for the Dutch West India Company, and by the 1640s had become governor of Curaçao, a Dutch-controlled island off the coast of Venezuela in South America. In 1644, he led an attack on the Portuguese on the island of St. Martin and during the battle lost a leg. Stuyvesant, with his wooden peg leg, would become a familiar sight in New Amsterdam in later years.

Peter Stuyvesant in New Amsterdam.

In 1646, Stuyvesant was made director general of the New Netherland colony. Stuyvesant did not believe in democratic institutions, although he did appoint a council of nine men to advise him. Many of the changes he made increased the power of the Dutch in the region. As a person, he was rigid and narrow-minded, and he was disliked by most people he dealt with. Many of his orders, such as a rule outlawing the sale of liquor to Native Americans, were simply ignored.

In 1664, New Netherland surrendered to the English. Stuyvesant went back to the Netherlands, hoping to retire there, but felt unwelcome in his homeland. He returned to America to spend the remainder of his life at his farm on Manhattan Island.

Dutch Fur Trade

The Dutch settlements were totally dependent on the fur trade for their money. Like the French, the Dutch relied on the native peoples for their trade. While the French allied themselves with the Huron people, the Dutch turned to the enemy of the Hurons, the Iroquois Confederacy. Thus the Hurons and the Iroquois became involved in increasingly bitter conflicts over the movement of goods between Europeans and Native Americans.

The Iroquois decided to move onto Huron territory in search of beavers, as the animals were becoming scarce on their own land. They also captured Hurons to replace members of their own tribe who had died of disease. After 1648, the Iroquois were armed by the Dutch. They continued to attack the Huron and any other Indian group who sided with the French. They then turned their anger on the French settlements along the St. Lawrence River, attacking and burning many to the ground.

In spite of their alliance with the Iroquois, the Dutch were very cruel toward the native people who lived close to their own settlements. The settlers cheated the Indians in business dealings, and in the mid-1640s began to murder them. This was because the Dutch wanted to seize Indian

Native Americans trade their furs for weapons and tools. The national rivalries and opportunities for trade that arrived with European colonists completely changed Indian groups and their relations with one another.

land for farms and to take control of the Native Americans' own trading system. Some of the Algonquin people, for example, traded corn from Long Island for furs from Maine, and the Dutch wanted this business for themselves.

The Dutch used their Iroquois allies and English forces to put down the Algonquins. The Algonquins fought back, but after three years of fighting were temporarily defeated. Hundreds of Indians as well as Dutch settlers were killed in the conflict.

Swedish Settlements

The Dutch West India Company felt particularly threatened by any rival colonies that sought to trade in fur. In the 1650s, they turned their attention to what they considered to be an annoyance in the Delaware River valley. In the late 1630s, Swedish settlers had established a small fur-trading post in the region that is now part of Pennsylvania, New Jersey, and Delaware. The colony was called New Sweden.

Although New Sweden never had more than 400 people, Peter Stuyvesant saw it as a threat to business. In 1655, he marched his soldiers against the Swedish settlers, who peacefully surrendered their colony to Dutch rule. During the army's absence, however, the Algonquin Indians attacked New Netherland once again, this time burning a number of scattered settlements and taking captives. Stuyvesant was humiliated and forced to pay a ransom for the Dutch hostages.

Settlers arrive from Sweden in 1638. New Sweden was a short-lived colony. It was founded in the 1630s and taken over by the Dutch in 1655. Among the settlers were Finnish people who had migrated to Sweden, petty criminals, and others who were unwanted in Sweden.

The End of Dutch Rule

Almost no one, not even the Dutch settlers, liked Dutch rule. It was harsh and at times brutal. The Dutch West India Company did not believe in freedom or democratic rule. Its directors wanted to control everything for their own advantage, and they had few allies. Company-appointed officials made laws and raised taxes from the residents of New Netherland. There was almost no representative government, and this was resented by many people.

In 1664, during a series of wars in Europe between England and the Netherlands, the English sent a naval force to conquer New Netherland. New Amsterdam was defended by a stone fort and 20 cannons, but the Dutch were weak after endless conflict with the Native Americans. When the English appeared, Stuyvesant surrendered without a fight. King Charles II put his brother, the Duke of York, in charge of the colony, and it was renamed New York. When the Duke of York became King James II in 1685, New York became a royal colony.

The Dutch in New York

The Dutch had a short and unsuccessful time as colonial rulers. Yet the Dutch presence is still felt in New York. During their time as rulers of the region, the Dutch put down roots that grew in later years.

Today, many towns and sites in the Hudson and Mohawk valleys carry Dutch names (Watervliet, Rensselaer, and Amsterdam, for example). This is also true in New York City. Two of its boroughs have Dutch names: Staten Island comes from the Dutch *Staaten Eyelnadet*. The Bronx is named after a settler called Jonas Bronck. Residents of the Bronx can visit Van Cortlandt Park, or cross into Manhattan over a body of water named Spuyten Duyvil. In Manhattan, the city's early history shows in street names and other names, especially Stuyvesant, that look back to the Dutch period.

People of Dutch ancestry have played major roles in American politics. Three presidents were descendants of early Dutch settlers: Martin Van Buren, Theodore Roosevelt, and Franklin Roosevelt.

Conclusion

In the years after 1492, Europeans began to dominate the Americas. A wave of immigrants first trickled and then flooded into North America from Europe and Africa. The native people who had lived in the Americas for thousands of years were transformed by these changes, just as they in turn changed the lives of the newcomers.

During the 1500s, the Spanish had the greatest influence on events. They brought with them things that were common to them but unheard of in the Americas: firearms, tools made of iron, horses, and new foods. They also brought their Christian religion and serious illnesses to which Indians had no resistance.

They took back to Spain gold, silver, slaves, and crops that Europeans had never seen before. These would alter European life forever.

The transfer of people, goods, ideas, and illnesses meant that the Atlantic Ocean was no longer the limit of the known world. Soon other European nations were challenging the Spanish for their piece of the American pie. By the mid-1600s, England, France, Holland, and Sweden had established settlements in North America. Some of these settlements would grow and change and push ever farther into the vast territories of the continent.

Life in the Algonquin village of Secota on the Virginia coast, as seen by John White in 1585. His drawings were of a civilization that was about to change.

Glossary

agriculture The work of farmers, mostly growing crops and raising livestock for food.

allies Groups, people, or countries that side together during a conflict.

archaeologists People who study human life and cultures of the past.

Archaic Indians Native Americans who lived in the period after the Paleo-Indians and developed diverse cultural traditions.

authority The power to make decisions and rules, or the people who have that power.

Calvinist Somebody who believes the teachings of the French religious reformer John Calvin, who taught that certain people are chosen by God to be saved, and the rest are sinners.

cash crops Produce from a farm, such as tobacco, that is grown for sale rather than for the farmer's own use.

commerce The business of buying and selling things.

confederacy An alliance of several groups that agree to act together and support each other.

democratic Describes a system in which people are their own authority rather than being ruled over by a king or queen. In a democratic system, people vote on decisions, or elect representatives to vote for them.

descendant A person who comes after another person in the same family. It can mean a son or daughter, or someone thousands of years later.

emigrate To leave the country of birth and go to live in another country.

exploit To make use of something. In the case of European settlers using other people's labor, it means using something unfairly or cruelly.

export To send something abroad to sell or trade. An export is also the thing that is sent, such as tobacco or cotton.

immigrant A person who has left the country of his or her birth and come to live in another country.

indenture A contract between a worker and employer, in which the worker agrees to work for a set period of time for no pay. In return, the worker's travel expenses, for example, are paid by the employer.

migrate To move from one place to another, sometimes back and forth depending on the seasons, and sometimes in search of food or a new place to live.

missionary	A person who goes to another country to convert the people there to his or her religion, and sometimes to help the poor or sick.
Muslim	A person who believes in the religion of Islam, which has Allah as its god and is the main religion in countries of the Middle East.
navigation	The skill developed by sailors to steer a course from one place to another in a ship. Today navigation is also used in air and space travel.
northwest passage	A sea route from Europe to Asia through the northern part of North America, sought by explorers for hundreds of years.
outpost	A base in a foreign country or in an outlying area that is used for military defense or for trading.
Paleo-Indians	Early hunters who probably migrated from Asia to North America in search of large animals.
parliament	A meeting of people to discuss and decide on public matters. The British government has two houses that together are called the Houses of Parliament.
plantation	A farm where crops, such as tobacco or sugarcane, are grown, and where the work is done by large teams of workers. In the past, these workers were often slaves.
pueblos	Indian villages in the American Southwest.
Puritans	Members of the Church of England who wanted to reform their church. They became a powerful force in England during the 1600s.
Reformation	The period in Europe in the 16th century when Christianity split into Roman Catholicism and Protestantism.
ritual	A set way of doing something for a ceremony or other act. Offering thanks to a god and preparing food in a certain way are both rituals.
Separatists	Puritans who wanted to leave the Church of England instead of trying to reform it from within.
technology	The knowledge and ability that improves ways of doing practical things. A person performing a task using any tool, from a wooden spoon to the most complicated computer, is applying technology.
tribe	A social group or community that shares traditions and ways of life. Native American tribes are part of larger groups called "peoples." These peoples often share a common language.

Time Line

c.13,000–10,000 B.C.	First humans probably migrate from Asia to Alaska. (Some historians believe this migration could have taken place much earlier.)
c.9000 B.C.	Mammoths and other large animals start to become extinct.
c.8000 B.C.	Archaic hunter-gatherer cultures begin to flourish in North America.
c.1500 B.C.	Corn cultivation begins in American Southwest and gradually spreads eastward.
c.500 B.C.	Burial mounds built by Eastern Woodlands peoples.
300 B.C.	Corn becomes important part of Native American diet in Eastern Woodlands cultures.
A.D. c.870	Vikings travel as far west as Iceland.
c.1000	Vikings reach Newfoundland, becoming first Europeans to sail to Western Hemisphere from Europe.
1096	First Crusade by European Christians to Holy Land.
1434	Portuguese navigators sail down African coast as far south as the northern Sahara Desert.
1444	Portuguese navigators reach Cape Verde Islands off coast of Africa.
1488	Bartolomeu Días reaches southern tip of Africa.
1492	Christopher Columbus lands on an island in the Caribbean.
1497	John Cabot searches for a northwest passage.
1498	Columbus lands on South American shore. Portuguese fleet led by Vasco da Gama reaches India after sailing around southern tip of Africa.
1512–13	Juan Ponce de León explores Florida.
1513	Vasco Núñez de Balboa becomes first European to see Pacific Ocean from America.
1519	Ferdinand Magellan begins voyage to sail around the world in a westward direction.
1521	Hernán Cortés overthrows Aztec empire and establishes Spanish power in present-day Mexico and Central America.
1527	Expedition including Álvar Núñez Cabeza de Vaca begins exploring Gulf Coast.
1534	Jacques Cartier makes first voyage of exploration for the king of France, exploring northeastern coast of Canada. King Henry VIII creates Church of England.

1539	Hernando de Soto begins exploration of eastern areas, starting in Florida.
1540	Francisco Vásquez de Coronado searches for Seven Cities of Cíbola.
1541	Third Cartier expedition attempts settlement in St. Lawrence River valley.
1565	St. Augustine, first permanent European settlement in North America, founded by Spanish in Florida.
1576	Martin Frobisher attempts to find a northwest passage.
1585	Sir Walter Raleigh founds an English colony on Roanoke Island.
1598	Juan de Oñate expedition establishes first Spanish settlement in the Southwest near present-day Albuquerque, New Mexico.
1603	Queen Elizabeth I of England dies and is succeeded by King James I.
1606	Virginia Company chartered.
1607	Jamestown, first permanent English settlement in North America, founded in Virginia.
1608	Samuel de Champlain founds French settlement along St. Lawrence River at the site of present-day Quebec, Canada.
1609	Henry Hudson explores northeastern United States for the Dutch. City of Santa Fe, New Mexico, founded.
1612	John Rolfe plants tobacco in Virginia, introducing a valuable cash crop.
1614	Dutch build Fort Nassau settlement near present-day Albany, New York.
1618	Powhatan dies.
1620	Pilgrims arrive at Cape Cod, Massachusetts, on the *Mayflower*.
1622	Virginia becomes a royal colony.
1626	Peter Minuit buys Manhattan Island from Native Americans and founds town of New Amsterdam.
1630	Settlers of the Massachusetts Bay Company arrive from England and found a colony in vicinity of present-day Boston, Massachusetts.
1633	Smallpox epidemic kills thousands of New England Indians.
1643	Dutch settlers massacre Native Americans.
1655	Dutch take over rival fur-trading colony of New Sweden.
1664	Dutch surrender New Netherland to the English, ending Dutch colonial rule in North America.
1673	Jacques Marquette and Louis Jolliet explore Mississippi River.
1681 –82	René Robert Cavelier, Sieur de la Salle, explores the Mississippi River as far as its mouth. Claims vast territory for France and names it Louisiana.

Further Reading

Brown, Margaret Wise, ed. *Homes in the Wilderness: A Pilgrim's Journal of Plymouth Plantation in 1620 by William Bradford & Others of the Mayflower Company.* Helotes, TX: Shoestring Press, 1988.

Bulla, Clyde R. *Squanto, Friend of the Pilgrims.* New York: Scholastic, 1990.

Cardona, Rodolfo and James Cockcroft, eds. *Juan Ponce de León: Spanish Explorer* (Hispanics of Achievement Series). Broomall, PA: Chelsea House, 1995.

Coulter, Tony. *Jacques Cartier, Samuel de Champlain, and the Explorers of Canada* (World Explorers Series). Broomall, PA: Chelsea House, 1993.

Dineen, Jacqueline. *The Aztecs* (Worlds of the Past Series). Old Tappan, NJ: Simon & Schuster Children's, 1992.

Johnston, Lissa J. and Álvar Núñez Cabeza de Vaca. *Crossing a Continent: The Incredible Journey of Cabeza de Vaca.* Austin, TX: Sunbelt Media, 1997.

Nichols, Peter and Belia Nichols. *Mastadon Hunters to Mound Builders: North American Archaeology.* Austin, TX: Sunbelt Media, 1992.

Sakurai, Gail. *The Jamestown Colony* (Cornerstones of Freedom Series). Danbury, CT: Children's Press, 1997.

Smith, Carter, ed. *Explorers and Settlers: A Sourcebook on Colonial America.* Brookfield, CT: Millbrook Press, 1991.

Websites

Town Creek Indian Mound – Used by the Muskhogean speaking Indians of the Pee Dee area approximately 300 years ago, this ceremonial burial site has been restored and offers a museum containing many relics of the past. www. sandhills.org/history/mound.htm

L'Anse Aux Meadows – The park has the first historic traces of a European presence in the Americas, the ruins of a Norse settlement from the 11th century, with wooden and earth houses similar to those found in Norway www.cco.caltech.edu./-salmon/wh-lanse.html

A Walking Tour of Plimoth Plantation – Plimoth (Plymouth) Plantation was the first permanent European settlement in southern New England (1620). archnet.uconn.edu/topical/historic/plimoth/plimoth.ht...

Bibliography

Binder, Frederick M. and David M Reimers. *The Way We Lived: Essays and Documents in American Social History*, 2nd ed. (Vol. 1: 1607-1877). Lexington, MA: Heath, 1992.

Boyer, Paul S., Clifford E. Clark, Jr., Joseph F. Kett, Neal Salisbury, Harvard Sitkoff, and Nancy Woloch. *The Enduring Vision: A History of the American People*, 2nd ed. Lexington, MA: Heath, 1993.

Carr, Lois Green. *Colonial Chesapeake Society*. Chapel Hill, NC: University of North Carolina Press, 1989.

Cronon, William. *Changes in the Land: Indians, Colonists, and the Ecology of New England*. New York: Hill and Wang, 1984.

Crosby, Alfred W., Jr. *The Columbian Exchange: Biological and Cultural Consequences of 1492*. Westport, CT: Greenwood, 1972.

Fiedel, Stuart J. *Prehistory of the Americas*, 2nd ed. New York: Cambridge University Press, 1992.

Foster, Nelson and Linda S. Cordell, eds. *Chilies to Chocolate: Food the Americas Gave to the World*. Tuscon, AZ: University of Arizona Press, 1992.

Hazen-Hammond, Susan. *Timelines of Native American History*. New York: Berkeley, 1997.

Josephy, Alvin, ed. *America in 1492: The World of the Indian Peoples Before the Arrival of Columbus*. New York: Vintage, 1992.

Kammen, Michael G. *People of Paradox: An Inquiry Concerning the Origins of American Civilization*. Ithaca, NY: Cornell University Press, 1990.

Marcus, Robert D. and David Burner. *America Firsthand: From Settlement to Reconstruction*, 2nd ed. (Vol. 1: Readings in American History). New York: St. Martin's Press, 1992.

Nash, Gary B. *Red, White, and Black: The Peoples of Early North America*. Upper Saddle River, NJ: Prentice-Hall, 1991.

Quinn, David B. *Explorers and Colonies: America, 1500-1625*. Rio Grande, OH: Hambledon Press, 1991.

Russell-Wood, A. J. R. *A World on the Move: the Portuguese in Africa, Asia, and America, 1415-1808*. New York: St. Martin's Press, 1993.

Thomas, Hugh. *Conquest: Montezuma, Cortés, and the Fall of Old Mexico*. New York: Touchstone Books, 1995.

Index